Good House Bad House

Understand how to make your house more Comfortable, Healthy, Safe, Durable, and Energy Efficient

By Matt Shipley

Published by
Maximus Press, Inc.

Good House Bad House, 1st Edition: Understand how to make your house more Comfortable, Healthy, Safe, Durable and Energy Efficient. No part of this book may be reproduced in any form or by any electronic or mechanical means including information storage and retrieval systems without permission in writing from the publisher, except by a reviewer, who may quote brief passages in a review.

This publication is designed to provide competent and reliable information regarding the subject matter covered. However, it is sold with the understanding that the author and publisher are not engaged in rendering home renovation, home performance improvement, or other professional advice. House construction varies from house to house and climate zone to climate zone and if home performance or other expert assistance is required, the services of a professional should be sought. The author and the publisher specifically disclaim any liability that is incurred from the use or application of the contents of this book.

Maximus Press Edition
Copyright © 2006 by Matt Shipley
All rights reserved.

Published by Maximus Press, Inc.

Maximus Press, Inc., PO Box 382, Ingomar, PA 15127

Printed in the United States of America

First Maximus Press Printing: April 2006

ISBN: 0-9774237-0-0
Library of Congress Control Number: 2005910040

Edited by Earnest R. Kuecher and Steve Osinski
Cover design and illustration by www.Stickman-Studio.com
Illustrations by Jason Battin

This book is dedicated to frustrated
homeowners everywhere.

Acknowledgements

First and foremost, I would like to thank the Department of Energy's Building America Program for providing the opportunity of working with great building science minds to advance the understanding of home performance. If it wasn't for them, I would never have obtained much of the knowledge I present in this book.

I want to express a deep appreciation to my friends and neighbors Shirley Crawford and Christie Galletta Horner for reading my early drafts and providing the insight I needed to alter my direction. I am particularly grateful to Earnest Keucher and Steve Osinski for editing the text and Jason Battin for the interior illustrations. Jason spent many hours learning about home performance issues and persistently drawing and redrawing illustrations until they portrayed the aspect and feeling I was trying to capture. An unrepayable debt goes to my cousin Daniel Burdette, a professional printer, for assisting me in selecting a printing company, guiding me through the printing process and resolving printing issues when I was unavailable.

I appreciate the artistic guidance and advice I received from my father, Michael Shipley, who has a master's degree in fine art from the Maryland Institute of Art. I also appreciate the assistance I received from the cover illustrator, Nathan Clement, for helping me create a more marketable book.

I owe a great deal to my wife, Christine, who helped edit, typeset and manage little matters concerning the book, all of which were vital to its publication. Finally, I would like to give special credit to our Creator who provided in me the interest, talent and will power to learn about this subject matter and write and publish this book.

Preface

Houses are the biggest investment most people make in their lifetime, yet very few people understand how houses function or perform. Consequently, builders are reluctant to build higher performing houses, which also cost more to build, because consumers will not pay more if they do not understand the value. Without understanding home performance or the way in which builders must build houses to make them perform better, home buyers often purchase houses riddled with performance issues. Tragically, after living in their houses, they become annoyed by seemingly unsolvable house defects and sometimes spend a lifetime trying to resolve them.

Two houses built side by side from the same floor plan but by two different builders could have a drastic difference in the way they perform simply due to the way they were individually constructed. Without knowing what to look for, home buyers could unsuspectingly purchase a new or existing house that will later cause deep disatisfaction. Hopefully, this book will alleviate that issue and, even if consumers decide to overlook the issues presented in this book, at least they can understand what they are giving up.

Since high school, I have researched house self sufficiency but I never found a book that described how houses work and what to look for in a well performing house. After buying my first house, based on criteria other than home performance, I settled into a long struggle of dealing with drafts, an underperforming conditioning system, high energy bills and mold. We hired companies to analyze our issues but none of them could fully explain or effectively improve them. It was not until I had the good fortune to work for a Building America residential research company that I was initiated into the building science realm and I came to understand why our first house performed so badly. During my tenure at the research firm, I not only was indoctrinated into cutting edge home performance research, I also was able to travel the United States talking and listening to builders from around the country. From this experience, I received a well rounded education on home performance, implementation issues and the need to help educate consumers.

As we head into an uncertain energy future, the cost benefit calculation for implementing the recommendations in my book will become more obvious. Even without rising fuel prices, having a well heated and air conditioned house with fresh air and low maintenance has a value beyond monetary terms. I have implemented many of the recommendations in my current house and our perceived comfort has risen immeasurably. Watching fuel prices increase and knowing that we can still economically remain comfortable in our home just adds more value to my efforts. Hopefully, readers of my book will be able to have the same experience!

Table of Contents

List of Illustrations

What You Don't Know Can Make You Uncomfortable

Nearly all of us have lived in a house with annoying and puzzling issues like cold rooms that should be warm, hot rooms that should be cool, pesky persistent drafts, musty-mildewy smells, mold or energy bills larger than what we should reasonably expect. By reading this book, you can solve many of these puzzling problems in your house or you can avoid the common construction pitfalls that lead to them.

In the first ten years of our marriage, my wife and I owned and lived in many houses that we considered Bad Houses in that they never fully met our comfort expectations. After numerous years of dealing with the different issues in each house, I learned what makes a Good House good and the defects that make a Bad House bad.

No matter how big, small, lavishly finished or inexpensively constructed your house may be, all houses should function in a similar fashion, unless of course, you have a house that defies the laws of physics. I say this because this book addresses the science of how houses work. Good Houses should keep you warm in the winter and cool in the summer, they should keep the inside air fresh and clean, and they should manage moisture so you do not need to worry about water damage or mold. Therefore, Good Houses keep the outside temperature conditions from affecting your indoor comfort and manage indoor systems to keep you healthy and safe. Furthermore, Good Houses should heat or cool every room in the house to your desired level of comfort without requiring you to resort to alternative devices such as space heaters or window air conditioners.

In contrast, Bad Houses do not do one, several or any of these things. If your house does not meet these standards, you may experience seemingly unexplainable annoying issues with your house. If your house does all these things well you will feel very comfortable and safe in your home.

You will find the information in this book invaluable because understanding what makes a Good House good will help you make better decisions about your current house or one you may want to purchase or build in the future. Unfortunately, you need to have many of the fine points that make a Good House good completed during construction or you will find them too costly to implement. Yet, you can still significantly improve underperforming existing houses to make them much more comfortable than they are now.

In this book, I focus on houses using wood stud framing, fiberglass insulation and central air systems because most US builders assemble houses using this type of construction. Understand that, builders *can* construct good houses at a reasonable price using this type of construction if they adhere to Good House principles. If they do not, you most likely will experience discomfort issues with your house.

Each chapter of this book addresses a different house performance issue you may experience. Frigid Lair covers the defects that cause rooms in your house to be cold in cold weather and hot in hot weather. Clogged Arteries explores how ducted conditioning systems are supposed to work and why they may not work so well. Next, Cold Feet walks you through the importance of and what to look for in well-insulated foundations. Then, Flueky Fireplaces enlightens how an open-hearth fireplace will actually cool your house down instead of warming it up. Hair Spray highlights the importance of fresh air ventilation and what to look for in a good ventilation system for your house. Mold and Musty Cellars explains how to control mold in your house by controlling moisture. Finally, Gas Chambers describes how fossil fuel burning appliances in your house and other sources of carbon monoxide can cause health problems for you and your family.

I have also included reference material that can aid you in your quest for a Good House. After reading this book, the Quick Reference Guide, Appendix A, can help you refresh your memory of the Good House details when looking at houses. It organizes the defects by type: Air Pathways, Conditioning, Insulation, Safety and Ventilation. For example, Insulation covers insulation type defects and Safety covers both mold and combustion type defects. Additionally, the Good House Inspection Check List, Appendix B, should help you to inspect houses in an organized manner. The construction glossary, Appendix C, will assist you with unfamiliar words and the Resource Directory, Appendix D, will help you locate products and websites referenced in the text. You can also scan through the Index to quickly locate a concept or section in the book.

This book should help you understand and recognize house performance issues as well as help you communicate to your builder or handyman how you want your house constructed or improved. For more specific detail on how to implement these recommendations, you should refer to the Energy and Environmental Building Association's Builder's Guide written for your climate zone. You can obtain a copy of this book from the Energy and Environmental Building Association's web page www.eeba.org. Additionally, if you need help deciding what to improve to get the most value for your money, you should contact a Home Energy Rater listed on RESNETs website:
www.resnet.us/directory/rater_directory.asp
Home Energy Raters can also help during construction by inspecting and measuring the performance of your house to ensure the builder meets or exceeds your agreed upon standards.

Enjoy using this book and if you have further questions, refer to the Good House website www.yourgoodhouse.com. At this site, you will find recommendations and links that will point you in the right direction.

Chapter One

Frigid Lair

If there is one thing my wife hates, it is being cold, and when she gets cold she lets me know about it! I sometimes lovingly refer to her as the "Squawker" because of the way in which she screeches my name to get my attention when I am in another room. She draws my name out in a way that makes a sound like a crow squawking by pronouncing the first letter 'M' as if she were enjoying a hot bowl of soup, Mmmm. Then she moves on to the 'a' which she draws out to sound like a sheep baaaaaing and she abruptly ends with a hard 'T', the entire time she increases the intensity of the letters as she pronounces them, 'MmmmaaaaaT'.

One very cold winter day she was sitting in our room above the garage and I was downstairs minding my own business when I heard my name squawked so loud it must have echoed through the neighborhood. I came to see what the squawking was about and I found her sitting there wearing gloves, a knit hat, sweatshirt and sweat pants with a blanket wrapped around her and her arms crossed to keep warm. She was upset because we could not keep her computer room comfortably warm. We had tried the usual things people do to keep a room warm; we added a space heater and put plastic over the windows but to no avail. Somehow the cold penetrated down to the bone. So, when all else fails, yelling the name of your spouse seems to be a viable solution: of course, my recommending that she go to another room did not help either of our situations.

Unfortunately, that room was also a problem in hot weather; so much so that we had to put in a window air-conditioning unit to keep it cool. Every spring I lugged the air-conditioner out of storage, installed it in the window and then did the same thing in reverse every fall. I can't tell you how many times I wondered why our central air system did not keep the room cool. Although I did not think of it at the time, rooms that get the recommended amount of heating or cooling and are still cold in cold weather will also be hot in hot weather. In other words, they tend to follow the outside conditions because the builder did not construct the house well enough to keep the heat in or out.

Looking back, I now understand the computer room had nearly every malady known to poor construction. The builders built it in such a way that the fiberglass insulation only provided half its rated value; in many places they installed too many wood studs in the walls where they could have installed insulation. Finally, air easily entered the room from outside which further reduced the room's comfort level.

To understand how to remedy or avoid having a house with a room or rooms like this, you need to first understand the individual components and concepts that come together in a house to keep the outside elements from affecting your inside comfort. I have listed these components and concepts, explaining why they are important, the defects that cause them and what you can do to prevent them.

Insulation

You will have a much more comfortable house by stopping heat and air transferring through your exterior walls from either direction. In nature, everything moves toward a balance so that hot will move to cold to make the inside and outside temperatures the same. Insulation slows down this process, and the more and better insulated your house, the slower this process happens. Of course, the more insulation you put into your house the more expensive your house becomes. When installed correctly, code-compliant levels of fiberglass insulation can adequately slow heat from transferring in or out of your house. When installed *incorrectly*, code-compliant levels of fiberglass insulation does not provide the comfort you should expect. As a matter of fact, incorrectly installed insulation can make you feel similar to how the Squawker felt in our house.

Insulation Cavity
In order for insulation to provide its rated value, it must completely and evenly fill the space between the exterior wall's studs from side-to-side, top-to-bottom and front-to-back (Illustration FL-1, pg 10). Any gaps or air pockets will make you feel uncomfortable. Tab-

less insulation batts work better than insulation batts with paper tabs, (Illustration FL-2a, pg 11), because they fit the space without disrupting the glueing surface of the studs or creating air pockets along the inside edge of the studs. If insulation installers use paper tabbed insulation they should choose the lesser of two evils and staple the tabs to the stud face. Illustration FL-2b on pg 12 depicts two vertical air pockets caused by nailing the tabs to the side of the studs. These air pockets help transfer heat in or out of your house and could cause condensation and mold in that area.

In our house, some stud bays were oddly spaced so that a gap existed between the fiberglass insulation and the studs. The installers further degraded the insulation value by stuffing it behind wall outlet boxes so air pockets existed between the outlet boxes, the insulation and the drywall (Illustration FL-3a & 3b, pg 13 & 14). Such gaps and pockets speed up the transfer of heat between the inside and outside of your house. These gaps and air pockets make it seem as if you do not have insulation in those areas because essentially you do not. Luckily for us, we were able to get at the backside of our walls to correct the situation in that location. Lucky as we were on that wall, we had many other walls we could not access without ripping them out, and we determined that it was not worth the effort or expense to fix.

Insulation Sandwich
Some attic walls typically do not have sheathing on both sides. This is an issue because fiberglass insulation by itself will not satisfactorily slow heat from passing through your house's walls; instead, it must work in conjunction with the sheathing material on either side of the framing. Only the complete wall system, with insulation sandwiched in between, slows heat passing through from either direction (Illustration FL-4, pg 15).

On the walls we could easily assess, we applied fiberboard sheathing like Energy-Brace® or Thermo-ply® to the back and taped the joints to sandwich the insulation. Drywall, OSB, or other types of sheathing work just as well, but fiberboard sheathing is light and flexible so we could more easily get it into tight spaces. Once we had the insulation installed and sandwiched correctly, our room upstairs showed a dramatic comfort improvement. If you have a house built, make sure the builder completely fills the exterior wall cavities and applies sheathing on both sides of your exterior walls, especially in rooms over garages or where houses have a space between the wall and your roof. If you already own a house, find places where you can access the backside of an insulated wall and determine if you can see the insulation. If you can see the insulation, cover it; it will make all the comfort difference in the world. Some other locations to look for insulation sandwiches include bump-outs, fireplace bump-outs, and bathtubs against exterior walls.

Bump-Outs

You need to pay special attention to houses that have portions of the house extended out past its foundation. From the inside, bump-outs or cantilevered floors look like bay windows that extend all the way down to the floor and from the outside they are suspended out past their supporting wall without columns or other support holding up the protruded edge. You can find bump-outs on the ground level or any other level above. Very commonly, you might find a bump-out floor without insulation or un-sandwiched insulation. Even when insulated, this area poses an air pathway problem often overlooked during construction. It is beyond the scope of this book to explain the specific details in relation to having this area well air sealed and insulated[1]. (For more detailed information about air sealing and insulating this area, refer to Cantilevered Floors in the Framing Chapter of EEBAs Builder's Guide for your climate zone, www.eeba.org.) Suffice it to say, if you have a house built, you want to ensure your builder applies continuous beads of glue on strategic wood-to-wood connections surrounding this area. They should also insulate the floor joist bay in the same manner described for an exterior wall and they should install bottom sheathing or rigid insulation with taped or sealed joints.

Fireplace Bump-Outs

Fireplace bump-outs are like other bump-outs except builders construct them for fireplace inserts so they can locate the chimney where it will not take space from the rooms above the fireplace. You will very commonly find fireplace bump-outs without insulation sandwiched in the walls or floor. This makes fireplace bump-outs even more of a problem than regular bump-outs for heat and air transfer. You will either lose or gain large volumes of heat and air from around your fireplace insert if you do not ensure you have an insulation sandwich covering all surfaces to the outside. If you build a house, check this area during one of your walk-through inspections to make sure the builder has covered this area with insulation and thin profile structural sheathing. If you own a house with a fireplace bump-out, look behind your fireplace insert to see if you have insulation sandwiched on the wall of the bump-out; if not, have someone come in and remedy the situation.

Bathtubs against Exterior Walls
Another common place you need to check for un-sandwiched insulation is between a bathroom tub and an exterior wall. During the construction process, builders will install bathtubs into a framed house before they start the finish work. This does not pose a problem unless you have a bathtub against an exterior wall where they rarely install sheathing material between the open end of the tub and the wall. You will find this most disturbing in the winter when your bathroom seems colder than the rest of your house and the bathtub itself transfers the cold. You will, of course, notice this even more if you have a metal bathtub instead of a plastic one. You can easily have this corrected during construction by ensuring the builder installs sheathing material between the tub and the exterior wall. You should be aware that accessing this area after the builder completes the finish work might pose a problem (Illustration FL-5, pg 16).

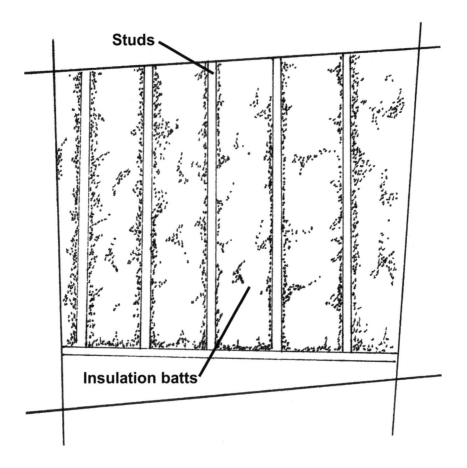

Studs

Insulation batts

FL-1 Completely Filled Stud Bays

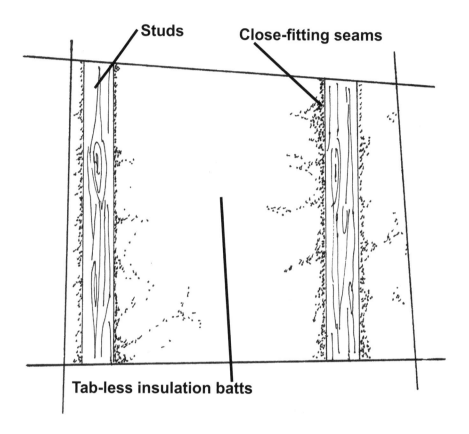

FL-2a Correctly Installed Tab-less Insulation Batts

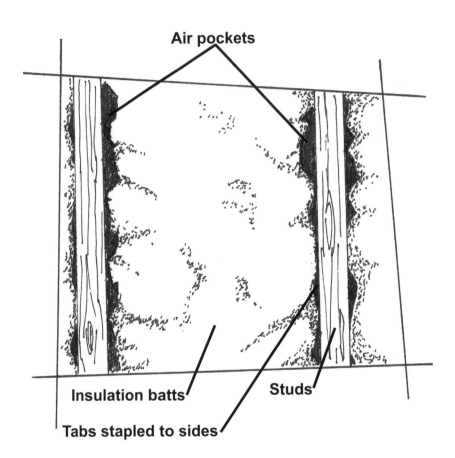

Air pockets

Insulation batts

Studs

Tabs stapled to sides

FL-2b Incorrectly Installed Insulation Batts

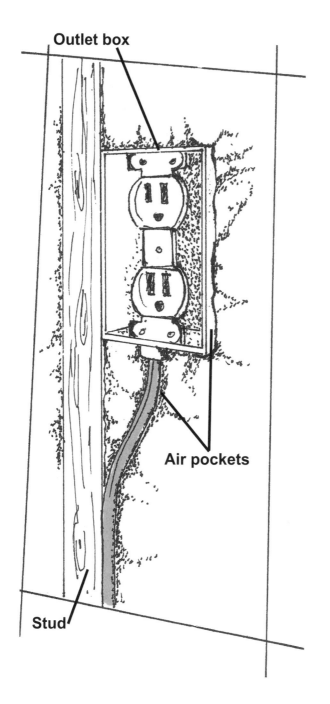

Outlet box

Air pockets

Stud

FL-3a Air Pockets around Outlet Box and Cable

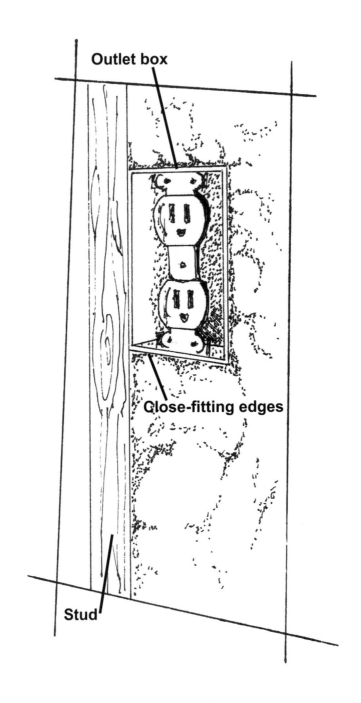

Outlet box

Close-fitting edges

Stud

FL-3b Correctly Installed Insulation around Outlet Box and Cable

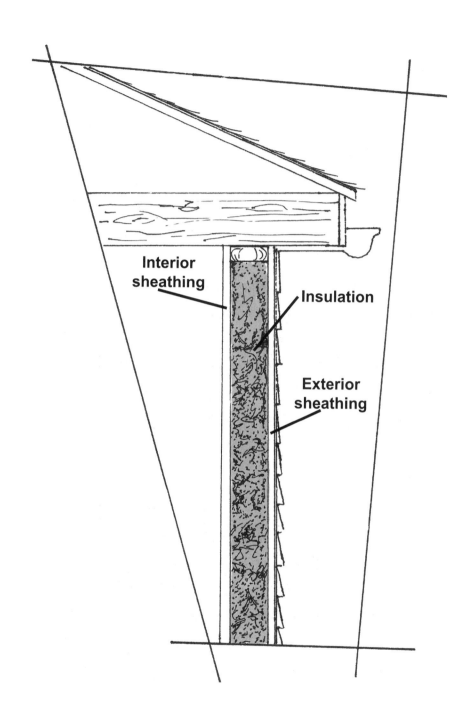

Interior sheathing

Insulation

Exterior sheathing

FL-4 Insulation Sandwich

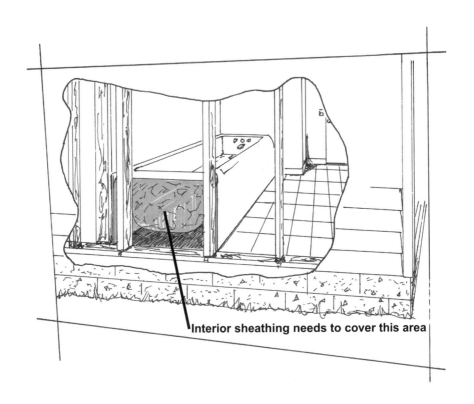

Interior sheathing needs to cover this area

FL-5 Insulation Sandwich Behind Bathtub

Wood as Insulation

Other than not installing the insulation correctly, builders can also reduce the insulation protection of your walls by installing too much wood. Wood is not a very good insulation material when compared to fiberglass insulation, and too much wood in exterior walls takes away space where the builder should install insulation. Our front coat closet was a good example of this; it sat in a corner of the house where two exterior walls came together and it was so cold in the winter that we could have turned off our refrigerator and used the closet instead.

Wood around Window and Door Frames

Builders sometimes install too many wood studs around window and door frames. In standard frame construction, depending on local building codes, the builder only needs one stud on either side of the exterior wall opening for non-load bearing walls. On load bearing walls, and in some non-load bearing walls, building codes require two studs on either side of the window or door opening. The two outside studs, called king studs, extend from the bottom plates to the top plates and the two inside studs, called cripple studs, can extend from the bottom plate to the window or to the door header. The cripple studs can support the window or door header which provides structure support for the wall or the builder can use joist hangers. Any other studs to the outside and up against the king stud are an unnecessary use of lumber and reduces the area in the wall where a builder could have installed insulation (Illustration FL-6, pg 20). Check your local building code requirements and ensure your builder installs no more studs than required by your local code.

Two-Stud Corners

If you own an existing home and you notice that corners of your house are colder than the rest of your house you may have too many studs in your corners. Once they finish building your house there is not much you can cost effectively do to remedy this situation. If, on the other hand, you have a house built, make sure your builder uses two-stud corners. Builders make two-stud corners by building two walls and propping them up to create a corner. Two-stud corners allow access for the insulation installer to install insulation all the way back into the wall so you will have warm or cool corners instead of cold or hot ones depending on the season (Illustration FL-7, pg 21). Builders often add a third stud to provide a nailing surface for drywall installers to attach drywall panels. Be advised that the third stud will not allow insulation installers to insulate all the way back into the corner. To solve this issue, they should use drywall clips to provide the nailing surface for attaching drywall.

Ladder Framing
Builders also install too many studs at the intersection of interior and exterior walls. They generally space studs in walls every 16 inches on-center. You will find that studs do not always line up where interior and exterior walls intersect, so builders install extra studs to provide a nailing surface for drywall on exterior walls (Illustration FL-8, pg 22). By doing so, they create potential air gaps and pockets when they alter the stud bay spacing because fiberglass insulation comes in 15-inch widths so they can snugly install it in the 14.5 inch stud-bays without modification. When builders install extra studs, they alter the 16-inch on-center spacing and create stud bays where insulation will not fit without manual modification. Yet, insulation installers can rarely modify the insulation well enough to snugly fill the space; and inadvertantly create air gaps in the wall where they used too much wood. As a result, you get a double defect, wood as a poor insulator and air gaps to help transfer heat faster.

Again, you can only remedy this by avoiding it during construction unless you want to tear out your interior drywall. If you build a house, have your builder install ladder framing at the intersection of interior and exterior walls. Ladder framing is nothing more than scrap studs cut and horizontally installed with the long side facing inward in the stud bay so insulation installers can install insulation behind them and framers have a nailing surface for interior drywall. They call it ladder framing because, when installed in stud bays, it looks like a ladder in your wall (Illustration FL-9, 23).

Thermal Bridges
Another framing-insulation error you may run into is where builders use steel studs in exterior walls. Metal is a good conductor of both electricity and heat; and if not insulated properly, steel studs

in your exterior walls will act like bridges for heat to transfer in or out of your house. The result will be a cold house in cold weather and a hot house in hot weather. Foam board insulation installed on the exterior against the studs works well to counter the effects of thermal bridging. If you want to use steel studs in your exterior walls, but do not want to experience the discomfort of cold and hot rooms or the displeasure of paying higher utility bills, ensure the builder installs code compliant levels of insulation on the exterior side of the studs to stop thermal bridging.

Attic Insulation

Finally, attic insulation caps the house off and keeps heat from quickly passing through your ceiling. This occurs in most houses; and it occurred in nearly all of our houses except one. Instead, that house had mounds of insulation in our attic that looked like an anthill farm. In many houses built today, builders use shredded fiberglass insulation, which is like the fiberglass in your walls except it does not come in rolls and installers generally blow it into your attic. This type of insulation works well as long as the installer completely covers the entire attic to the required depth. To apply the insulation, installers usually stand in your attic access with a hose and blow the insulation into your attic like a fireman putting out a fire. Since installers may find it difficult to accurately judge the depth of insulation at all locations in your attic, they instead estimate the depth and it is usually to the detriment of your comfort. Some spots in your attic may have more insulation than others and other spots may have significantly less insulation than what you need to stay comfortable in your house. To avoid having an attic ant hill farm, make sure they have completely covered your attic to the depth required by your local code[2]. You will also find it very helpful to have depth gauges placed around your attic so that you and the insulation installer can judge the depth at different locations while standing in the attic doorway[3] (Illustration FL-10, pg 24).

Now, I am very lucky to have the Squawker in my life. In addition to alerting me to honey-do problems, she runs our household in nearly every other way. Since I am often on the road, she runs our finances, cleans our house, takes care of our pets and she also does some very impressive home improvement projects like knocking out walls and putting in closets. She is irreplaceable to me, so I don't mind too much when she squawks, because I know it is for a good reason. Besides, she keeps me focused to make sure I explore every possibility, like when she knew that incorrectly installed insulation was only half the problem in our upstairs room. She could feel something else was wrong.

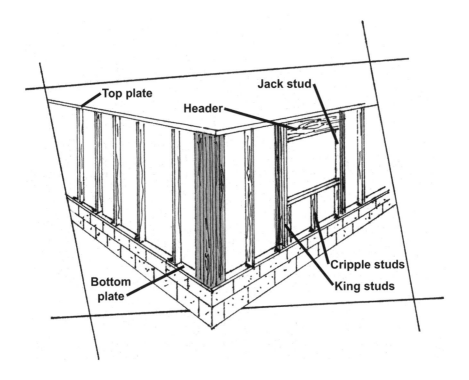

FL-6 Excessive use of wood in exterior walls (highlighted studs)

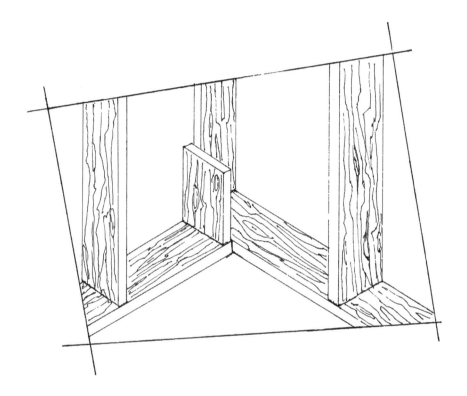

FL-7 Two-Stud Corner

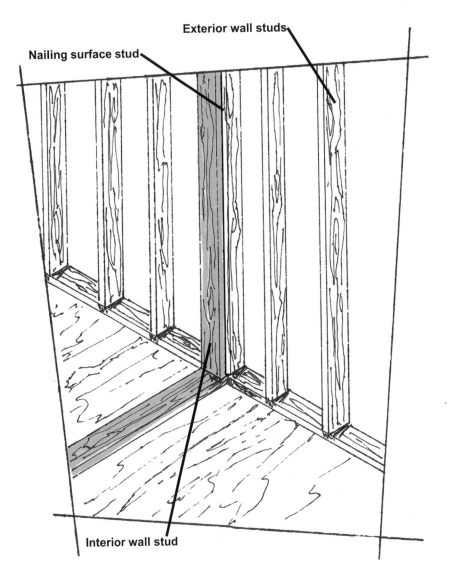

Nailing surface stud

Exterior wall studs

Interior wall stud

FL-8 Altered Stud-Bay Spacing

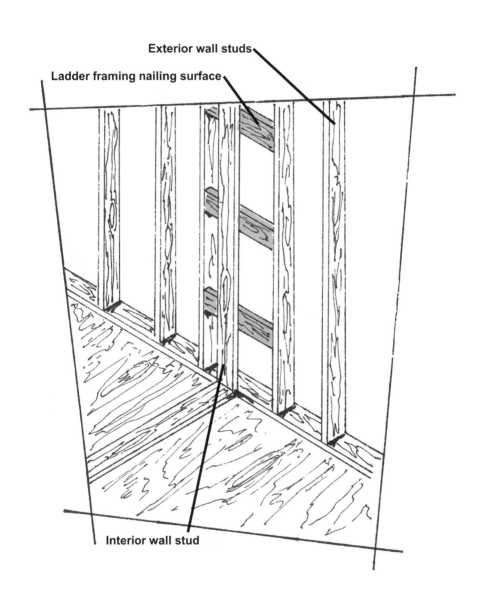

Exterior wall studs

Ladder framing nailing surface

Interior wall stud

FL-9 Ladder Framing

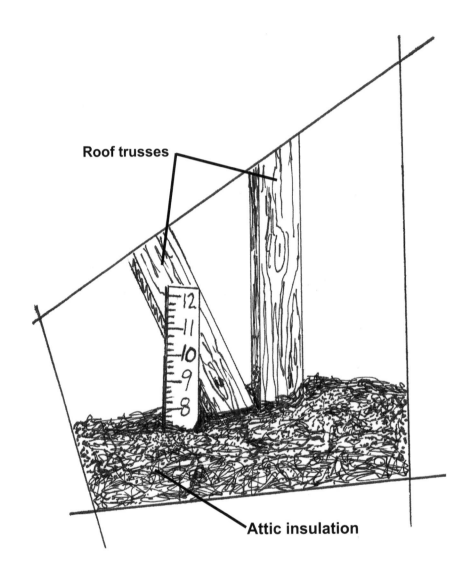

Roof trusses

Attic insulation

FL-10 Depth Guage

Air Leakage Pathways

It turns out the Squawker was right, because heat will pass just as quickly through your walls via small seemingly insignificant holes and cracks as it will through poorly insulated walls. This time airflow is the culprit. If air can flow through a wall, heat will go with it as well as moisture and other things you do not want in your house or would rather not breathe. All the fiberglass insulation in the world will not do you much good if you have air leakage pathways in your house. For example, cold weather is not too bad without the wind blowing; but when a freezing wind blows through closures and seams in your otherwise warm clothing it feels as if your warm clothing is no longer keeping you warm. This effect is so powerful that weather forecasters created the wind chill factor to describe its effect in measurable terms. Although your house cannot suffer from the wind chill effect, you can suffer from it in your house. The increased air infiltration will lower indoor humidity and make you feel colder because moisture will more freely evaporate from your skin, just like the effect caused by wind chill. To stop heat loss and counter the wind chill effect in your house you need to seal areas where air can flow through your exterior walls, floors and ceilings.

Drywall as an Air Boundary

Housewraps, which I will further discuss in the Mold chapter, installed shingle style, up the side of your house are your house's first line of defense against air penetration. Yet, air still gets past the housewraps and into your exterior wall stud bays. Your house's air stopping last line of defense is your interior drywall finish. When sealed to studs, drywall makes an excellent barrier to air trying to get in or out of your house. When not sealed, air slips around edges of the drywall because builders rarely put continuous beads of glue on studs before they attach drywall to them. The glue acts like a rubber gasket on an airtight jar but will only work if the drywall installer has glued all 4 edges of each drywall sheet to the studs (Illustration FL-11, pg 31).

Outlet and Light Switch Air Pathways

Air also gets past drywall through outlets and light switches in exterior walls. Air will enter your wall stud bay in any number of places from outside to find a hole or crack to the inside wherever it can. For example, air can enter one stud bay and travel to others via the holes drilled in studs for wires and cables. Outlet and light switches then provide an easy path for air to get into your house because common outlet and light switch boxes do not seal out air and they extend through your interior drywall finish. If builders use gasket outlet and light switch boxes they can eliminate this air pathway into your house. Gasket boxes seal air out by having rubber gaskets for wires to penetrate into the boxes. You can achieve this same effect by spraying foam insulation into cable access holes in non-gasket existing outlet and light switch boxes. You can have this done during construction or you can do it afterwards. If you do it yourself, turn off the electric to your exterior wall outlets and switches from the circuit breaker. Next, remove the outlet and light switch plates on exterior walls, then install insulation spray foam in the hole where the electric cables come into your outlet or light switch boxes. If you do not have any other seams or gaps in your outlet or light switch boxes this will seal the boxes as well as or better then gasket boxes.

Recessed Light Air Pathways
Other air pathways through your drywall that contribute to air leakage are recessed lights, especially ones installed between conditioned and unconditioned spaces like your attic. Lights generate heat, which they must dissipate or they could cause a fire. Most recessed lights have small slits in the top to allow heat from the light to escape, but this slit also allows your conditioned air to escape. In fact, when you turn on the light, heat from the light actually helps drive air out of your house (Illustration FL-12, pg32). To solve this issue you can install, or if accessible, replace existing recessed lights with airtight recessed lights. Airtight recessed lights have a larger area on top, so heat from the light can dissipate inside the light's module (Illustration FL-13, pg 33), and wires leading into the light go through a rubber gasket, which also seals the air path.

Window and Door Air Pathways
Other major draft-causing culprits in any house are windows and doors. Although I highly recommend purchasing the most energy efficient window on the market when constructing a house, I

personally cannot justify the expense when you have otherwise perfectly good windows in your existing house. Besides, much of the air from your windows and doors most likely infiltrates between the window or door jam and the rough opening of your house. If you carefully pull off the window or door trim from the interior side of your window or door, you will see the window/door jam and the rough opening of your house. Many builders stuff fiberglass insulation in this gap in an attempt to stop heat from transferring through it; but they cannot stop heat transfer if they do not stop the air and fiberglass insulation only acts as a filter to air that passes through this gap. By removing the fiberglass insulation and applying low expanding foam in the gap, you can air seal and insulate this area as well as reduce the draftiness of your windows and doors (Illustration FL-14, pg 34).

Builders and window manufacturers do not recommend this practice because of the high incidence of over-exuberant foam installers putting too much foam in the gap between your window jams and rough openings of your house. Too much foam, when it expands, may bow the window casing causing the windows to malfunction, which becomes a warranty item for the window manufacturer or builder. Without foam in the air gap you will have an annoying draft which you will be tempted to blame on your windows, so don't let their quality control issue become your comfort issue. Installing foam correctly is not difficult, it just takes a little skill and practice. So don't be timid about asking your builder to install low expanding spray foam insulation or pull the insulation out and install it yourself.

Cable and Wire Air Pathways
Along with the increase in technological innovations comes another hole drilled into your house to run a cable or wire to a computer, TV or other device. These small intrusions into your conditioned spaces may seem insignificant, yet combined they can equal the area of a small open window. To counteract this invasion you should make sure you also spray expanding foam into the hole after the installer runs the wires or cables through. This applies to any penetration through your exterior wall, floor or ceiling where the hole leads to an unconditioned space or to the outside (Illustration FL-15, pg 35).

Bottom and Top Plate Air Pathways

Air can also enter your house where your exterior wall meets your floor. Builders attach walls and floors by connecting studs from the bottom of the wall to the plywood or concrete floor. The studs at the bottom of an exterior wall is called a bottom plate and the one at the top is called a top plate. These wood-to-wood and wood-to-concrete connections do not make an airtight seal and since the interior drywall does not cover these seams, it does not stop air from coming in or out. To air seal these seams, builders need to either apply a continuous bead of glue or install a gasket under the bottom plate and on top of the top plate (Illustration FL-16, pg 36). Gaskets work much better for wood-to-concrete connections because they also act as a capillary break, which stops moisture from transfering from the concrete to the wood.

Foundation Wall Sill Plate Air Pathway

The purpose of the foundation wall sill plate is to level the foundation wall and to keep untreated floors and band joists out of contact with concrete. Moisture transferring to wood from concrete could cause them to rot. For the same reasons described above, your foundation wall sill plate will allow air to pass and that is why builders also need to install a foam sill gasket underneath foundation wall sill plates (Illustration FL-16, pg 36). The sill gasket not only stops air from entering your house in this area, it also stops moisture from transferring from the foundation wall to the sill plate. Unfortunately, they must do this during construction because you cannot cost effectively install it later.

Band Joist Air Pathway

Band joists are belt-like pieces of lumber that run the entire perimeter of your exterior house to cover the ends and outermost sides of your floor joists. You find band joists on houses that sit on basements, crawlspaces or have more than one floor. You can more easily see the inside of a band joist in an unfinished basement or a crawlspace by looking where the floor joists stop on top of a foundation wall (Illustration FL-17, pg 37). Most builders only stuff fiberglass insulation into band joist bays to help thermally protect them; but again, the fiberglass insulation will not do anything to stop air from coming through. Fiberglass insulation needs sheathing material on either side to stop airflow and provide the advertised R-value of insulation. You can cut rigid foam insulation boards to fit in each joist bay as blocking and then seal the seams on all four sides with a continuous bead of glue. This can be time consuming and potentially expensive depending on material and labor costs. As an alternative, I recommend you have industrial type spray foam, such as Icynene® or CorBond®, sprayed into each band joist bay. The foam both insulates and air seals your band joist as well as reduces the likelihood of pests infesting or populating your band joist bays.

One of our houses had fiberglass insulation stuffed in the band joist, but I was reluctant to remove it because I was unsure of the cost and I had other home performance projects higher on my list. I decided the fiberglass insulation had to go when I noticed rodents tunneling into it to make a nest.(Illustration FL-18, pg 38). I located a local Icynene® installer on the web and called them for an estimate. I was pleasantly surprised at how little it cost to have my entire interior perimeter spray foamed. In no time at all, I tore out all the fiberglass insulation from the band joist and as I was doing that I discovered an infestation of carpenter ants. I called our pest control company and they came and treated our house before the spray foam installer foamed our band joist.

Fiberglass insulated band joists make an ideal nesting location for rodents and insects. Rodents can burrow into fiberglass insulation, shredding it as they make a cozy little nest. Wood eating insects can bore through your band joist from outside to colonize the space between your band joist and your fiberglass insulation. Rodents will not find foam insulation near as convenient to create a nest and insects will not tunnel through foam if treated with an insecticide such as boron.

Had the builder installed spray foam in the band joist when building the house, we would not only have had a more comfortable and efficient house from the start, it would most likely have prevented the rodent problem. If the builder had also used boron injected spray foam, it may have prevented the carpenter ant infestation because you can control insects such as wood destroying organisms like carpenter ants and termites with boron derivatives. Boron is a natural element mined from the earth which is non-toxic to humans and pets and is frequently used, in boric acid form, as an insecticide.

More Detailed Information

Builders use a variety of methods and materials to construct foundation and exterior walls, so my objective in describing major air pathways in most houses is for you to get a general understanding of them. For more specific air sealing technique information on your particular wall assembly, refer to the EEBA Builder's Guide for your climate zone, www.eeba.org. In the Builder's Guide you will find page after page describing different types of wall assemblies.

Although, the Squawker and I made incremental improvements on our uncomfortable house, we ended up moving to a house that had fewer defects to improve. You can make significant improvements to some houses and others you will just have to live with what you have. If you know what to look for, you can make better decisions before you buy a house that you may later find uncomfortable. If you hire a local Home Energy Rater to inspect your newly or previously constructed house, they can provide an evaluation of how well your house will perform and what you can do to make it better.

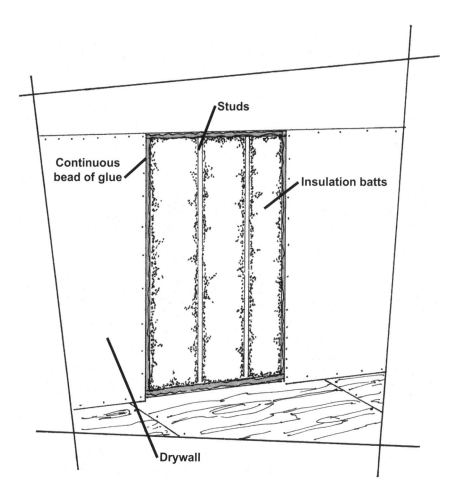

Studs

**Continuous
bead of glue**

Insulation batts

Drywall

FL-11 Drywall Air Boundary

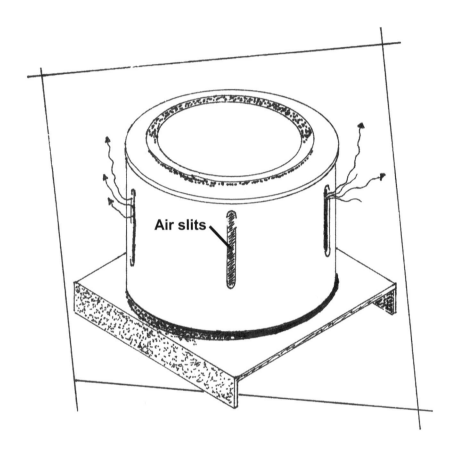

Air slits

FL-12 Standard Recessed Light

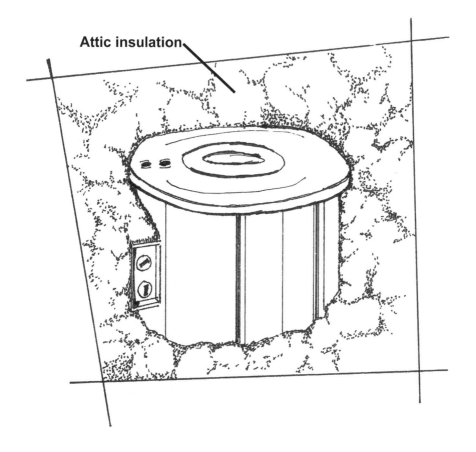

Attic insulation

FL-13 Airtight Recessed Light

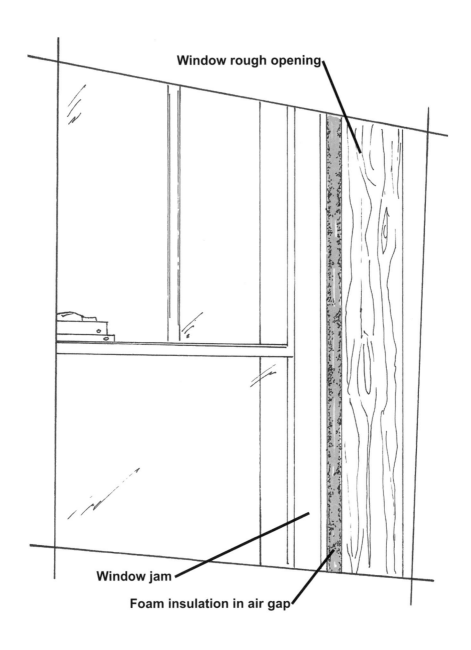

Window rough opening

Window jam

Foam insulation in air gap

FL-14 Window Air Gap

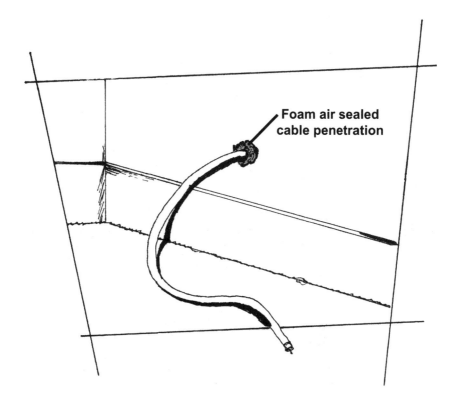

Foam air sealed cable penetration

FL-15 Cable Air Pathway

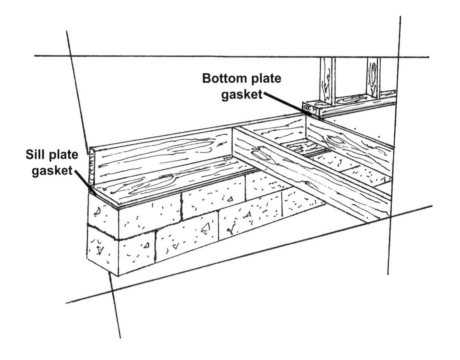

Bottom plate gasket

Sill plate gasket

FL-16 Bottom Plate and Sill Plate Gaskets

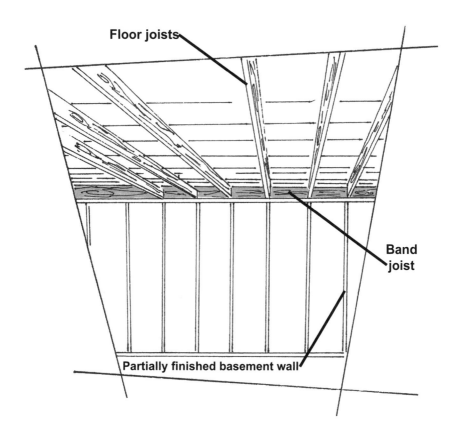

Floor joists

Band joist

Partially finished basement wall

FL-17 Interior View of Band Joist

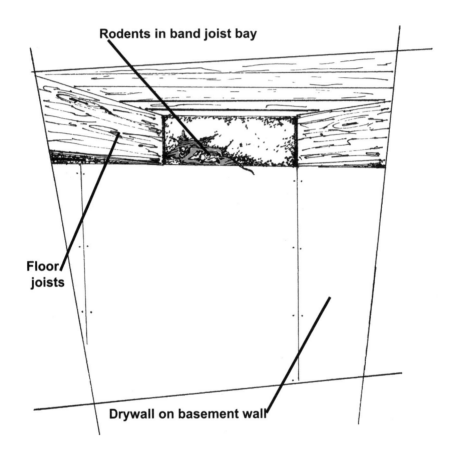

FL-18 Band Joist Bay Rodent Refuge

The Squawker likes to sit in our den and crochet while watching television. She gets settled in nice and cozy on our sofa with one of her afghans covering her legs while she sits there wearing her fleece jacket and listening to her entertainment news programs as she crochets a new afghan. It is the very picture of tranquility until our air handler kicks on and the vent above her head blows cold air down her neck. Well, as you could guess, she again lets out a squawk, MmmmaaaaaT! This time she has me crawling through our attic looking for what is going wrong. Of course, I did not figure it out at the time so she gave in to desperation and had our heat pump replaced with a gas furnace, which did not solve the problem, but, at least, she took action.

Like most houses, our houses had central air systems that blew conditioned air into rooms via a maze of air ducts. No matter how high or low we set the temperature on the thermostat, we had rooms that never seemed to get warm or cool as they should. In addition to stopping heat and air from transferring through your walls, ceilings and floors you must also have a conditioning system that works properly in order to feel comfortable in your house. A malfunctioning conditioning system is what was ailing the Squawker, although at the time we could not figure out why.

Conditioning System Operation
A central split-system heat pump has three main components: an outdoor condensing unit, an indoor air handler and an air duct system (Illustration CA-1, pg 41). The condensing unit heats or cools refrigerant, which it pumps to the air handler that cools or heats the air and blows it into the main duct. The air duct system channels the air to rooms and, ideally, returns the same amount of air back to the air handler. In many ways, central air systems resemble a body's circulatory system in that they condition air in one location and pump it throughout the house and return an equal amount of air to the air handler via air ducts that act like arteries and veins. The amount and final temperature of hot/cold air

pumped into rooms determines how well your system heats or cools each room.

In the process of delivering the correct amount of air to rooms, the conditioning system conditions air by making it either hot or cold and then drops it into the air handler. The air handler acts like a heart by pumping the conditioned air into the house's main air duct, which functions like a main artery to carry the air to smaller air ducts for distribution around the house.

Just like arteries that get smaller and more numerous as they reach their destination, so do supply air ducts. They do this to regulate the amount of air that goes to each room. In general, larger volume rooms require more air, so either the system uses larger air ducts or more branches feed into that room. Smaller volume rooms require less air so smaller ducts supply those rooms.

Once air enters a room through a diffuser or register (Illustration CA-2, pg 42), it must mix evenly with air already present in the room in order to bring (or maintain) the entire room temperature up, down, or constant to the occupant's desired level of comfort. The system completes the circulatory loop when the house's veins or return duct system returns air to the conditioning system to recondition and re-circulate air to rooms.

Conditioning System Issues

Now that we better understand the way the system should work, let me explain why the Squawker didn't get the conditioned air she wanted when she wanted it. First, most builders do not have the system designed well from the start; then air duct installers further compromise performance by squeezing ducts between framing, piping, wires and other unforeseen obstacles. Finally, air ducts by their nature leak air.

System Design Defects
Many builders do not have the system designed well from the start because they may have a difficult time accurately determining the amount of air needed to heat and cool each room.

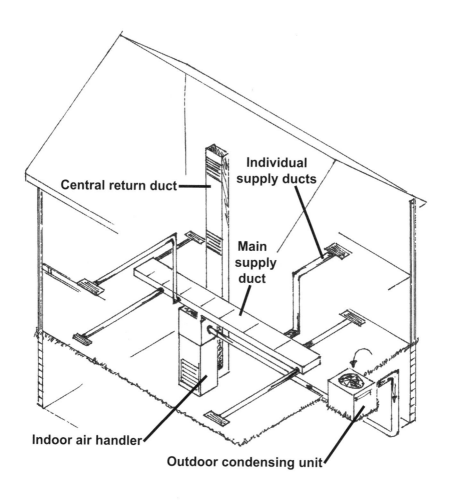

Central return duct

Individual supply ducts

Main supply duct

Indoor air handler

Outdoor condensing unit

**CA-1 Central Split-System Heat Pump
Conditioning System**

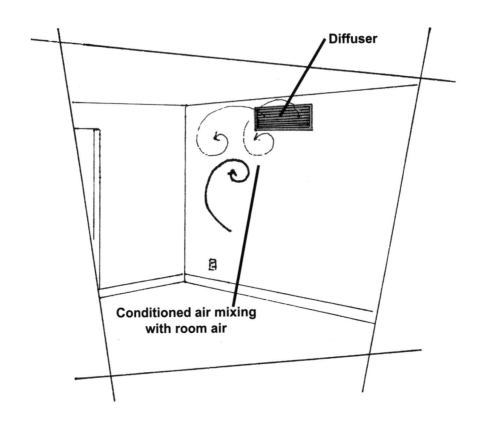

Diffuser

**Conditioned air mixing
with room air**

CA-2 High Side Wall Diffuser

Each room requires a different amount of air based on the volume of the room, the surface area of the windows, the insulation value of the windows, the amount of insulation in the external walls and the cardinal orientation of the room, i.e., north, south, east or west facing. Before building a house, builders must take each one of these factors into consideration for each room when designing the central air system to cumulatively calculate the total amount of air needed for the house. From this, duct system designers determine airflow requirements for each room to design duct runs. All ducts have resistance to airflow, so the longer the air duct the less air it will deliver at the end of it. Fittings that redirect airflow cause significantly more resistance to airflow then do straight pieces of duct. To compensate for this, duct system designers must mathematically add the equivalent length airflow resistance of these fittings to the total length of duct runs as if they were straight pieces of air duct. In this way, they can calculate how much air they will lose due to resistance in duct runs and calculate how much air they need to force into ducts at the beginning to have the prescribed amount at the end. Unfortunately, many builders do not do this in the way I just described; instead they estimate the total volume of air in a house based on the total square footage of the house or the combined square footage of the rooms. Then they estimate the house air tonnage requirement based upon that and do not have each duct run designed for rooms they supply. As a result, air duct installers do not have a properly calculated airflow target or a plan laid out for getting the right amount of air to each room.

Installation Defects

Not correctly calculating each duct run only compounds the errors made by air duct installers. Without knowing each room's air requirement, air duct installers will not be able to size the ducts and fittings based on this more precise airflow target. They instead must use their skill and experience to estimate each room's air requirement and they usually do not accurately calculate the resistance to airflow in each air duct run. Too often, the result is a central air system that delivers too much air to one room and not enough to another; and a house in which you could be very cool in one room and very warm in another.

Installing and adjusting balancing dampers that vary the resistance to airflow in each air duct branch may correct some of this. HVAC servicemen mostly use balancing dampers to adjust individual airflows which always result in less total airflow even when used to increase airflow in a particular room. Even when a room's airflow improves, adjusting dampers only reduces the margin of error of airflow to each room instead of creating a system that delivers the right amount of air to the right room. That is why I say it is better to have a system designed and constructed for performance than to worry about how you can make an inadequate system marginally better.

Leaky Ducts
Leaky ducts can further reduce the amount of air going to your rooms and, on average, can account for between 15%-30% of your heating and cooling costs. Some ducts leak more than others but every type of air duct leaks. Often, you can attribute much of the air leakage found in systems to a single disconnected or partially disconnected duct. This is especially true for systems in which HVAC contractors use cloth duct tape to hold ducts together. For this reason, air ducts are the one thing in your house for which you should not use duct tape.

Not all duct leakage is the same, as some types of duct installation techniques cause more leakage than others. To better understand how leaky ducts affect your comfort and utility bills, you must understand the difference between duct leakage to the outside and inside of conditioned spaces, as well as leakage between supply and return air ducts. Of the four types of duct leakage, you will find that supply duct leakage to the outside will affect both your comfort and utility bills more than any other type. Duct leakage to the outside most commonly occurs when you have supply ducts in attics, unconditioned crawlspaces, exterior walls and common walls between your house and your garage[4]. As described before, your air handler forces conditioned air into your supply ducts for delivery to your rooms. As a result, the pressurized conditioned air in your supply ducts will push through any gaps in your ducts to the outside atmosphere. Essentially, supply ducts in unconditioned spaces are helping to heat or cool the outside. Your conditioning system must make up for that lost air so it will draw outside air in through air pathways in your house. Consequently, you don't get the air needed to adequately condition your rooms and your conditioning system must work harder to condition the outside air drawn in to make up for supply air duct loses.

Next, in descending order of severity, you have return duct leakage to the outside caused by return air ducts located in unconditioned spaces. In this case, your return air duct does not have pressurized air like the supply air duct so instead of forcing air out, it draws outside air into the duct and delivers it to your air handler. Your conditioning system must work harder to condition this air which also causes higher utility bills. Aside from utility bills, this will only minimally affect your comfort because without any other types of significant duct leakage, you will still have most of your conditioned air delivered to your rooms. Some people may reason that this is a good way of introducing fresh air to your house, yet I personally do not want to breathe dusty, insulation-particle infested air that comes from an attic, unconditioned crawlspace or exterior wall.

Finally, the last two types of duct leakage, interior supply and return leakage, cause the least problems because the majority of energy you put into conditioning your house will stay in your house. Of the two, interior supply duct leakage will make you feel less comfortable because it diverts conditioned air to other locations in your house instead of to the rooms in which you want it. Conversely, interior return duct leakage causes your conditioning system to draw air from the outside through air pathways in your house to make up for the air it does not return back to your air handler. This is minor compared to exterior return leakage, yet it will still affect your utility bills. To summarize, exterior supply leakage is worse than exterior return leakage, both of which are far worse than either type of interior leakage. Interior supply leakage will make you less comfortable whereas interior return leakage will raise your utility bills.

Air Tempered Ducts in Unconditioned Spaces
Although our builder inadequately designed and installed our air

duct system, the Squawker's complaint mostly stemmed from the fact that our supply air ducts ran through unconditioned spaces. In addition to the pressure effects on your house that I just explained, the outside temperature will also temper air in your ducts. In houses with supply ducts in unconditioned spaces, some conditioned air from inside the duct leaks to the outside and what does not leak is tempered by the outside climate as it flows through ducts in unconditioned spaces. In our case, the Squawker was being hit on the head by air tempered with our cold attic air. That is why, in our house of infinite defects, we suffered most from the cold attic air cooling down our conditioned air as it passed through un-insulated attic supply ducts. As an extra added bonus, we also had the pleasure of paying extremely high utility bills while we sat there freezing.

If you have supply air ducts in your attic, you can moderate their ill effects by air sealing and insulating them. First, make sure you seal the seams as described in the next topic, Air Duct Sealing. Then, construct a trough around the duct, and fill the trough with loose fill insulation (Illustration CA-3, pg 47). Ensure you allow at least six inches of space between the side of the trough and the duct. Finally, ensure the trough extends at least six inches above the duct to sufficiently insulate the top of the duct. If the builder ran your duct through an exterior wall or common wall between your house and your garage, there is not much you can cost effectively do to improve this.

Air Duct Sealing

No matter how hard you try, you will never completely stop air from leaking out through duct-to-duct and duct-to-fitting connections. Given this fact, don't let this stop you from significantly reducing air loss in air ducts to within an acceptable level which will greatly increase performance of your house's conditioning system. If builders do a good job sealing air ducts, ducts should lose less than 10% of the total air handler airflow measured via a duct blaster test. They should air seal ducts wherever two ducts fit together or where a duct and a fitting come together by applying either UL 181 approved water based mastic or tape. Any other type of mastic or tape than UL 181 approved will not hold its seal over time.

For existing ducts you can try AeroSeal®[5]. AeroSeal® duct sealing system injects adhesive particles into your air duct system. The particles travel through your air ducts seeking holes and cracks located throughout your duct system. The adhesive duct sealing particles attach directly onto the edges of any hole and crack, effectively sealing it without coating the inside of your ducts. To measure results of this technique have a Home Energy Rater take a before and after duct blaster test and determine an improvement by comparing the two.

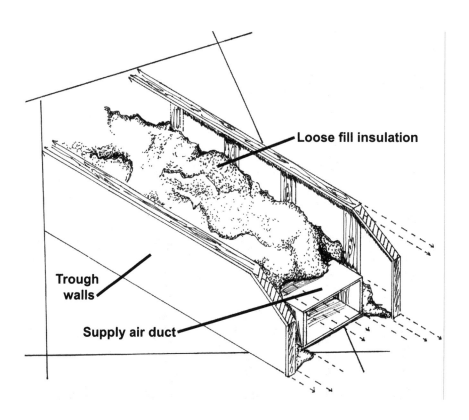

CA-3 Supply Duct Insulation Trough

Panned Air Ducts

If you want to know how well the conditioning system works on an existing house, you can get a good idea by checking to see if the builder installed panned air duct returns. Panned air duct returns are a sure sign of a cheaply constructed conditioning system. Builders create panned returns by nailing a piece of sheet metal to the bottom of floor joist cavities (Illustration CA-4, pg 50) or by putting drywall on either side of studs of vertical wall cavities (Illustration CA-5, pg 51). Panned returns are inefficient because of how much they leak. A little leakage in your return system will not cause much trouble as long as you have the ducts within conditioned spaces and you have an airtight house. Unfortunately, panned returns rarely just leak a little, they actually leak the most of any type of duct; and you will find them nearly impossible to seal to an acceptable leakage rate. If you have a choice, you should avoid them in any house.

Floor Diffusers

Most floor diffusers you find in homes are artifacts from days when residential systems were not used for cooling. They were designed to direct hot air into the center of rooms before it rose straight up to the ceiling. Consequently, they are terrible for cooling your house. In order to gain better summer cooling performance, you should replace these floor diffusers with diffusers that have individually adjustable vanes so they can diffuse air in the winter and throw air straight up in the summer.

Furniture

As previously explained, builders install diffusers to diffuse or throw air into rooms so it can mix with existing air in the room to bring or maintain the entire room temperature up, down or consistent with your desired level of comfort. Oddly enough, your interior decorator can also affect the performance of your central air system by placing furniture to block diffusers. When you put furniture in front of, or over diffusers, air from the diffuser cannot adequately mix with air in the room to accomplish its comfort task (Illustration CA-6, pg 52). If you want your conditioning system to function optimally then try not to block diffusers when placing furniture in your house.

You may not always have this option, because builders locate most diffusers low on a wall or on the floor under a window; the same place you find ideal to put a sofa, chair or table. Our den has a big long sofa in front of one of our diffusers, and although I move the sofa away from the diffuser as much as space will allow, I know that I am still restricting my central air system from working to its optimum ability. If I had built our house, I would have had the builder install the diffusers high on interior walls where I would need to go out of my way to find something to block them. But, I did not have our house built and we live with what we have.

Pressure Imbalances

Every central air system creates a pressure environment in your house caused by the force of air blowing into your rooms. This does not pose a problem unless your system malfunctions and causes a pressure imbalance. Even with all your room doors closed, your entire house should be at the same pressure. Pressure imbalances can cause your conditioning system to work harder and draw make up air from outside through air pathways into your house. This in turn causes increased utility bills and a reduction in your comfort.

Centrally Located Return Ducts

Central returns are a cost effective way of installing return duct systems that work very well as long as air from all rooms can make it to the central return unimpeded by closed doors. Central returns are less expensive to install because air duct installers do not need to run individual return ducts to each room. If you close a door and air has no other way to flow back to the central return, air pressure will build up in the closed room. This air pressure will make it difficult for the air handler to pump more conditioned air to that room and consequently make the room less comfortably conditioned. You can determine if a house has a central return by identifying a very large return grille located roughly in the center of your house; most commonly in a hallway. Additionally, you will notice that individual rooms do not have return grilles.

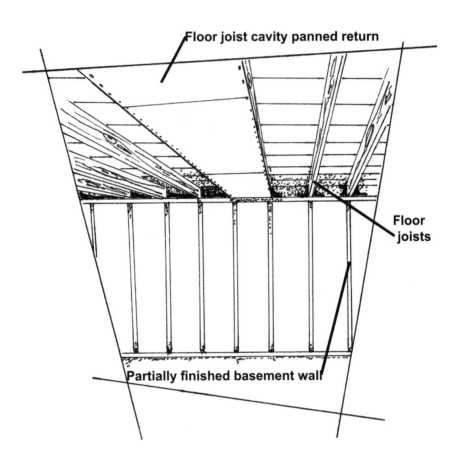

Floor joist cavity panned return

Floor joists

Partially finished basement wall

CA-4 Floor Joist Cavity Panned Return

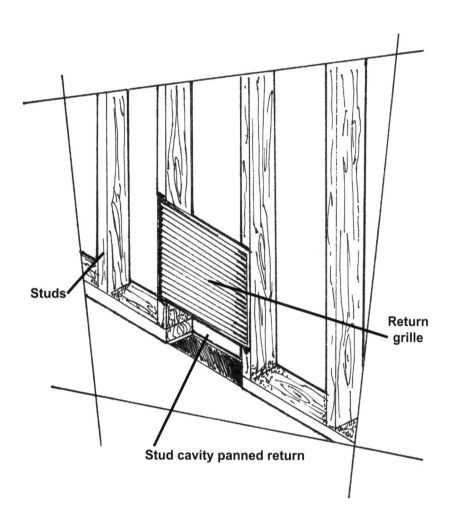

Studs

Return grille

Stud cavity panned return

CA-5 Stud Cavity Panned Return

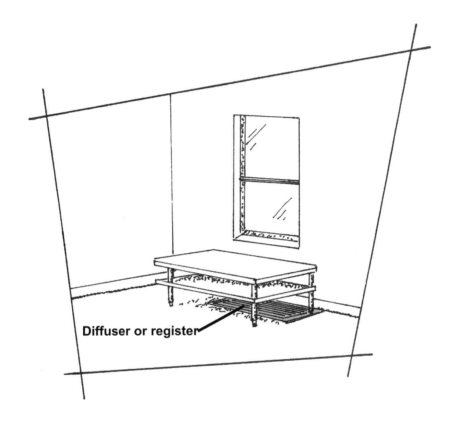

Diffuser or register

CA-6 Furniture Blocking Diffuser or Register

Jump and Transom Ducts

If you have a central return system and your house does not have jump or transom ducts in rooms with doors, when you close one of those room doors the air blown into that room will need to force its way under the door to make it back to the return. If you have wall-to-wall carpet, this issue often manifests itself on your carpet by leaving a dirt strip underneath the door. In this capacity, your carpet acts like a filter for air flowing underneath. The opening under your door is not wide enough to allow enough air to get back to the air handler, so the air handler must draw air from outside to make up for air lost in the closed room or rooms. By now, you should know this will increase your utility bills.

You can alleviate this problem by having either jump or transom ducts installed in your house. Jump ducts are ducts that link air in a room with air outside the room by a duct that jumps up into the ceiling, over the wall and back down into the hallway or area on the other side (Illustration CA-7, pg 55). Transom ducts are ducts that link air in a room with the air outside the room via a grille that goes through the wall into the room (Illustration CA-8, pg 56). You will find that jump ducts transfer less sounds from rooms, so if you want more privacy in a room you should install a jump duct. While transom ducts will transfer most sounds from rooms, they cost less to install and you don't need to worry about insulating and air sealing them since they stay inside your conditioned spaces. Functionally, both jump and transom ducts work well, so it is your choice of which one to install. If you have a central return without them, your system will not function to its peak performance and you will pay a higher price in utility bills.

Conditioning System Analysis

If you build a house with a duct system, make sure your builder knows the required airflow for each room based on all factors listed in this chapter and has a plan to get air to each room. Builders should have a floor plan that shows the types of ducts, where they run, the duct fittings and the amount of resistance in each duct to deliver the required amount of air to every room. Builders should also have an unimpeded path for air in your rooms to get back to your air handler. Where possible, ensure ducts run inside conditioned spaces of your house and the installer properly seals them.

If you already own a house with a duct system and it does not perform well, check to see if you have furniture blocking the diffusers or if you have ducts that run through unconditioned spaces. Also, contact a Home Energy Rater to perform a duct blaster test to determine the air leakage of your system. If you have furniture blocking your diffusers, ducts running through unconditioned spaces or excessive leakage, take the steps described in this chapter to improve them. A Home Energy Rater can also help you if you don't have these issues and you still do not get enough air to a room or rooms in your house. All these defects have an effect on each other, which can lead to similar issues like rooms that do not meet your comfort expectations. Make sure you analyze your house as a system to determine the main cause of an issue or issues you experience. As a last resort, adjusting your balancing dampers may partially solve your problem.

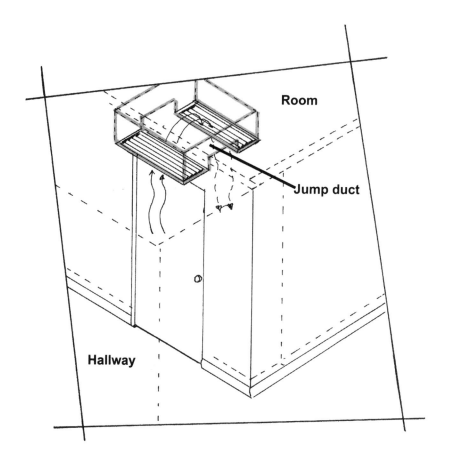

Room

Jump duct

Hallway

CA-7 Jump Duct in Attic

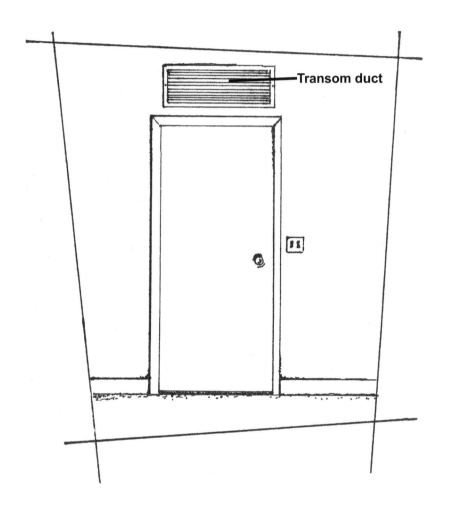

Transom duct

CA-8 Transom Duct above Door to Room

Cold floors will not affect your sleeping habits unless your spouse gets cold feet like mine does. Most every cold winter's night, as I settle into a peaceful slumber, my wife stealthily slides into bed so as not to disturb me. Then she puts her frigid feet against my legs causing me to yell and jolt into the air. I angrily tell her to keep her feet away from me, but she complains that her feet are so cold and my legs are so warm and I should share the warmth. After the initial shock, I usually calm down and allow her to put her feet close to my skin, but I still do not like it. I suffered the most from this ritual when we owned a house built on a crawlspace.

Crawlspaces

Crawlspaces are open areas between the ground surface and the bottom of the main floor with less than normal headroom. Most US building codes require crawlspaces to have vents installed to the outside, ostensibly to allow moisture to escape, but the open vents do not control moisture in your crawlspace as intended. A side effect of vents is that they make your crawlspace the same temperature as the outside. This, coupled with our lack of insulation in the crawlspace, made our floor cold enough to use as an ice skating rink in the winter. The Squawker's feet would quickly become icy cold from walking around our house. My options were simple, I could either get the crawlspace air sealed and insulated or I could convince the Squawker to wear snow boots as bedroom slippers. Given that the second option would have led to a further lack of sleep on the sofa, I opted for air sealing and insulating the crawlspace.

Originally, I tried stuffing fiberglass insulation up into the floor joist bays with the insulation paper facing up to retard the moisture transfer from my house to the crawlspace[6]. This helped, but it didn't stop the air leakage and the insulation was not as effective because I did not sandwich it between two sheathing materials. I could have sandwiched it by using a flexible sheathing material and if my crawlspace opening had been larger, I might even have done it. Then, I discovered that treating my crawlspace like a short basement would better resolve my sleeping problem. Some types of construction, such as houses on pier pilings, will preclude your treating your crawlspace like a short basement because they do not have walls. In this case you can easily get sheathing material into your crawlspace to sandwich insulation in your crawlspace floor.

You might find it less expensive to construct your crawlspace like a short basement because it will take less materials to insulate and air seal it than if you tried to sandwich the insulation in your floor. Insulated crawlspace walls will make the air inside your crawlspace remain at a similar temperature to the air in your house, just like a well air sealed and insulated basement. Also, you will better control moisture in a basement-like crawlspace than in one open to outside air.

You can create a basement-like crawlspace by air sealing and insulating your crawlspace walls, which includes the air vents. You can increase the insulation effectiveness of your walls by installing the insulation on the outside (Illustration CF-1, pg 59). This allows your walls from being directly effected by outside temperatures, so less heat transfers in or out. To complete the thermal protection of my crawlspace, you should foam spray your band joist to seal the air pathway. For extra added thermal protection, you can install foil faced rigid insulation on the bottom of the floor joists with the foil facing down to act as a radiant barrier. By doing all this, I greatly improved the extreme cold feet syndrome and dramatically improved my sleeping habits.

Before I could air seal and insulate my crawlspace, I first needed to gain control of moisture accumulating there. Moisture accumulating in your crawlspace can lead to, among other things, excessive mold growth, and by closing off your crawlspace without controlling moisture you will make the situation much worse than if you had just left it vented. For these reasons, my primary concern became controlling sources of moisture in my crawlspace. Moisture most commonly gains access to your crawlspace via evaporation from the ground and crawlspace walls, and via air pathways like your crawlspace vents and band joist. You can also get water in your crawlspace via leaking pipes, a rising water table or water run off.

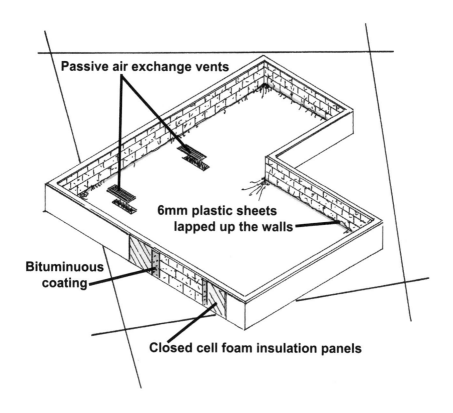

Passive air exchange vents

6mm plastic sheets
lapped up the walls

Bituminuous
coating

Closed cell foam insulation panels

CF-1 Cut-Away View of Crawlspace Wall

Crawlspace Moisture Control

Ground Moisture

The biggest source of crawlspace moisture is the dirt or sand floor through which ground moisture will evaporate into your crawlspace. You can easily take care of ground moisture by covering the entire crawlspace floor surface with 6mm thick plastic, overlapping and sealing the plastic seams, and lapping the plastic six inches up on the side of the walls, and pier pilings if your house has them. Moisture will also penetrate through your crawlspace walls and foundation if you do not have them adequately protected. Ideally, you want to install a drainage plane system that sheds water from your crawlspace walls and foundation to your foundation drainpipe and away from your house, as I will more thoroughly explain in Musty Cellars.

Leaky Pipes, Flooding and Water Run Off

Since your objective is to keep moisture and bulk water out of your crawlspace, you should ensure you do not have any manmade sources of water in your crawlspace. You should check for any leaks from pipes, or vents that may discharge water into the crawlspace and reroute them to the outdoors. Sometimes, excessive rain will cause your crawlspace to flood via a rising water table or water from the outside draining into your crawlspace. To protect your crawlspace or your basement from rising water tables, you should install a sump pump system that drains to the outside away from your house and in a downhill direction. You also need to check for sources of water flowing toward your foundation and redirect its path away from your house. If you cannot divert water runoff away from your house, you should also install a sump pump to evacuate water that makes it way into your crawlspace from this source.

Crawlspace Vents

By sealing off your crawlspace's external vents, you will seal off another source of crawlspace moisture, because humid summer weather may vent more moisture into your crawlspace than it vents out. When outside air has 100% humidity, the air venting into your crawlspace will have the same amount of humidity. If you have effectively controlled other sources of moisture in your crawlspace, closing and blocking your vents with insulation will improve your crawlspace moisture conditions.

Moisture Conditioning

By allowing air to exchange between your crawlspace and house, your house's conditioning system will help regulate the remaining moisture content in the crawlspace when you air condition your house. By including your crawlspace in your conditioning system, you will mix any moisture accumulation in there with the rest of the air in your house so moisture will be less likely to affect your crawlspace. You can better control moisture in your crawlspace by installing a supply and return duct there. In this way, you will actively add your crawlspace to your house's conditioning space to regulate its moisture and keep your floors warm or cool depending on the season. Under certain mild humid conditions, by doing this, you will still have a potential for condensation on top of the plastic ground covering; but, this risk is minimal compared with other methods of controlling moisture in your crawlspace.

After you have controlled moisture in your crawlspace, you can concentrate on improving its thermal condition. To achieve this you will need to insulate your crawlspace.

Foundation Insulation

Exterior Crawlspace Insulation

You can keep your crawlspace or your foundation wall better insulated by having the exterior of it insulated with closed-cell foam insulation[7]. Exterior insulation isolates your crawlspace or foundation wall from fluctuating outside temperature conditions. As an added moisture control measure, you might also want to apply a bituminous tar type coating on your exterior walls before installing closed cell foam panels to protect your wall against any moisture or water that finds its way behind the foam panels. For this reason you also need to have sheet metal flashing[8] installed at the top to help divert water from finding its way behind the panels. The sheet metal flashing will help prevent termites which burrow up through foam insulation from gaining access to your wood sill plate. To accomplish this you must install the flashing between your foundation wall and sill plate (Illustration CF-2, below). Due to the termite problem, you will find code restrictions in some areas against exposed insulation on your exterior crawlspace or foundation wall. Yet, with the sheet metal flashing installed properly, you can apply for a code variance.

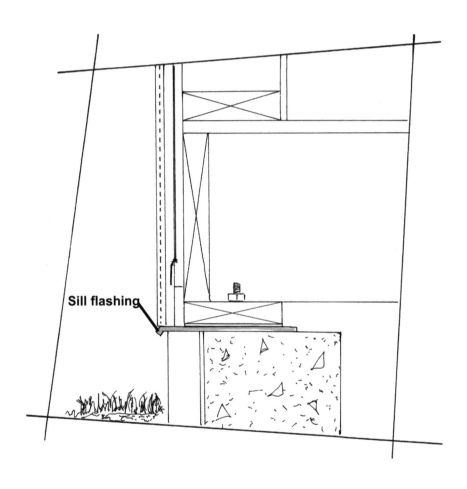

CF-2 Sill Flashing for Exterior Foam Insulation

Interior Crawlspace Insulation

You can insulate the interior of your crawlspace wall as long as you do not have excessive moisture coming through your wall. If you have excessive moisture coming through your wall, you need to rectify that situation first as explained above. Even if you do not have excessive moisture coming through your crawlspace or foundation wall, you will always have some moisture transferring through it. To counter this effect, ensure you use a type of interior insulation that allows moisture coming through your walls to also pass through the insulation. Otherwise, insulation will trap moisture between it and the wall which could lead to excessive mold growth. Perforated insulation blankets such as CertainTeed's Basement Wall and Masonry Wall Fiber Glass Building Insulation work well for this purpose. You can hang them from the sill plate and the perforations will allow moisture to transfer through the insulation into your crawlspace where your conditioning system should take care of it. No matter what type of foundation insulation you use, exterior or interior, you should find it much easier and less expensive than insulating and sandwiching your crawlspace floor joists.

Crawlspace Access Doors

Whether you choose exterior or interior insulation to insulate your crawlspace, you must still insulate and air seal your crawlspace access door. If you have an un-insulated and non-air sealed crawlspace access door, you will counter the effectiveness of your wall insulation. Air and outside temperature conditions will permeate into the rest of your house from your crawlspace if you don't have a weather-stripped and insulated crawlspace access door.

Other Types of Foundations

Floors above basements or floors on concrete slabs could cause similar effects to your comfort like the multi-faceted threat created by crawlspaces. No matter what type of foundation your house has; crawlspace, basement or concrete slab-on-grade, you should have your foundation insulated or your floors will be cold. If the builder did not air seal and insulate your basement or crawlspace, then your floors will be cold. If your concrete slab does not have insulation around the edges, then it too will be cold.

By insulating your exterior slab you can decrease the amount of dust mites and other micro-organic life that would otherwise thrive if you did not. If your slab is colder than the rest of your house, it will have a higher moisture content, which creates ideal conditions for micro-organism growth. If you can help increase the temperature of your slab, you can decrease the relative humidity at that surface, which decreases the ideal conditions for micro-organism growth. Finally, if you live in a cold climate, you may want to have insulation underneath your foundation slab which provides extra thermal protection for your concrete floor.

The Squawker and I enjoy fireplaces. The soft warm glow, the smell of burning wood and the crackling sound of the fire filled our hearts with warmth. Unfortunately, that was the only thing that it filled with warmth unless we stood or sat close to the fire itself. While we sat there thinking that we were reducing our utility bills, the utility company sat back laughing at us.

Fires use air to burn, and our fires were pulling the comfortably warm conditioned air from the rest of our rooms, using it to fuel itself, and sending the remnants up the chimney (Illustration FF-1, pg 66). I always wondered why the rest of our rooms seemed colder when we burned fires. Our house replaced the warm conditioned air in the rooms with cold outside air. The replacement air came in through air pathways, or unsealed air passages in our exterior walls, ceiling and foundation. This also made our heating unit work extra hard to make up for lost conditioned air and caused our heating bills to be extra high. This happens whenever you have an open flame in your fireplace without a direct source of outside combustion air, regardless if you use wood, gas or other type of fireplace fuel.

If that wasn't bad enough, dealing with the smoke and ash was. Many times when I started a fire, it did not generate enough heat to cause smoke to go up the chimney. Instead, air would come down the chimney and blow smoke from the fire into our house. The smoke caught me there, red-eyed and coughing with the smoke alarm going off, the cats running from the noise and the Squawker nowhere to be found; she had seen it too many times. I needed to open a door and a window so the cross ventilation would get the smoke out, which made our house even colder.

The fireplace didn't just cause problems when burning fires; it also caused them when it just sat there idle. Even with the damper in the flue closed, heat from our house would escape up the chimney and cold air would blow down it. This not only robbed us of the heat that we paid to pump in, but it blew ash all through our

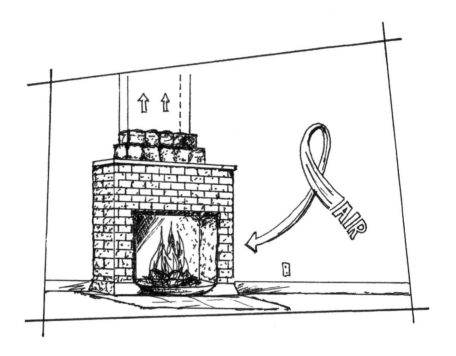

FF-1 Open Hearth Fireplace

house so we had a fine film on every surface. It was enough to convince me I needed to remedy all my fireplace issues.

Some open-hearth fireplaces have dedicated outdoor air combustion intakes to alleviate a few of these issues, but, among other things, they do not stop the draft caused by the chimney. In order to solve the entire problem you must completely isolate your conditioned air from the combustion process in your fireplace. Russian wood burning stoves and regular wood and pellet burning stoves with a combustion air port from the outside will accomplish this.

Russian wood burning stoves are full masonry fireplaces with the combustion chamber fed from the outside. In this way, the fireplace uses outside air for combustion and you get the benefit from the fire as it warms the masonry walls and radiates heat into your house. Russian wood burning stoves are usually totally encapsulated by stone, so you will not be able to sit in your house and enjoy your fire unless you have a portion of the wall left open and install sealed tempered glass between you and the fire. The tempered glass will also help speed the heat transfer when you first start a fire. A major drawback of Russian wood burning stoves is that they are very expensive to build because you must have them constructed on location one stone at a time.

Wood and pellet burning stoves are a less expensive option and come in a variety of styles from different manufacturers. Whether you purchase a wood or pellet burning stove, you should obtain one with outdoor air combustion intakes to draw the combustion air from outside instead of from inside your house. You will find that pellet burning stoves have a more complete combustion process so you get a very efficient burn and less pollution goes up your flue to the atmosphere. When you burn logs in your wood burning stove, the incomplete combustion process releases hot gases up your flue which produces a greater amount of atmospheric pollutants and results in a less efficient burn. Some wood burning stove manufacturers offer a secondary combustion chamber for hot gases so you get a burn comparable to pellet stoves. You can also buy wood stoves made with stone. Stone wood stoves will retain heat better than steel stoves and release it into your house over a longer period of time.

I was very interested in a stone wood burning stove but the thought of cutting and storing wood, dragging it through our house and dealing with the mess did not appeal to me. To completely solve all my fireplace issues I purchased a direct-vent gas fireplace insert and had it installed. Gas fireplace manufacturers make direct-vent gas fireplaces by completely sealing them from the interior of your house with a piece of tempered glass and importing combustion air through an air duct from outside and exporting exhaust via another air duct to outside. In this way the Squawker and I were able to enjoy the warmth and glow of fires without the dust, mess and hassle of dealing with an open-hearth fire. We only missed the smell of wood burning and the sound of fire crackling. Given the fact that I didn't need to spend many evenings and weekends chopping wood, transporting it to the fireplace, or cleaning up a mess from the wood and ash, I was more than happy to forgo the smell of burnt wood and the sound of a crackling fire. Besides, if it were that important to me, I would buy a crackling fire CD and an atomizer filled with the essence of burning wood to spray in our house while I play the CD and enjoy our gas fireplace.

If you have ever experienced the choking displeasure of breathing your spouse's hair spray that hangs in your house like a lingering cloud of smog, then you are truly unfortunate. It is the kind of odor that makes me want to open windows in the dead of winter to flush air out of our house. If you are fortunate enough to have forgone this displeasure, you may alternatively have suffered from similar annoyances caused by other aerosols or the aromatic scent of brand new wall-to-wall carpet. Additionally, if you are among those who think home air fresheners freshen your air, then you might be disappointed to find they actually increase pollutant levels in your house. Those of you who put your faith in popular ionic room air cleaners may also be disappointed to find they do not provide the recommended fresh air you need. Odors linger in your house longer than necessary because your house most likely does not exchange air frequently enough to keep your inside air fresh and clean.

Houses Do Not Need To Breath but People Do

Even if you do not smell unpleasant odors, your house's air may be more polluted than recommended. Builders unintentionally ventilated houses built prior to the 1970s energy crisis by the numerous air pathways they did not seal in houses. Since then, in a quest for consumer comfort, energy efficient builders have made houses more airtight without installing systems to properly ventilate them. Recently, research shows that your indoor air can have two to five times more pollutant concentrations than outdoor air. People spend approximately 90% of their time indoors and a significant portion of that time in their own homes so it now has become more important than ever to have well ventilated houses.

Recommended Air Exchange

No matter what type of ventilation system you install, the American Society of Heating, Refrigerating and Air-Conditioning Engineers (ASHRAE) recommends almost all houses must have a whole-house mechanical ventilation system rated at 7.5 cubic feet per minute (cfm) per person plus 1 cfm per 100 square feet of floor area. This amounts to an air exchange of 50 cfm for a 2000 square foot house with four occupants[9]. At this rate even leaky houses will not provide the recommended amount of fresh air exchange.

Ventilation Systems

Types of Mechanical Ventilation

Mechanical ventilation can come in three varieties: balanced system, exhaust-only and supply-only. Balanced systems employ both supply and exhaust fans to draw air in and out of your house at a near equal rate, hence the name balanced. Exhaust-only fans pull air out of your house without an installed air vent for drawing it in. (Illustration HS-1, pg 71) Supply-only fans draw air into your house through a dedicated air vent attached to your return system. Just as the name implies, they only have an installed method for bringing air into your house and not one for venting it out.

Balanced System Ventilation

Since, each of these systems has certain drawbacks; you must make a decision on which system will best suit your situation. Balanced systems are difficult to balance properly and require a special AirCycler™ controller on your central air system. In cold climates you may find the energy costs of this strategy very high if you do not have some method of heat recovery from your exhausted air and if your furnace does not have an electronically commutated motor. The AirCycler™ controller on your central air system will turn on your air handler fan at regular intervals to cycle the air through your house even when you have your heating or air conditioning turned off. In this way it can stir your house's air so that you don't have stagnate air staying at the bottom while air at the top vents out.

Electronically commutated motors (ECM) cost more to buy, yet, they will save you money over their service life because they operate more efficiently than other motors. Over half of all electrical energy consumed in the United States is used by electric motors. During a cheaply made motor's service life you can pay up to 50 times more in operational costs than the original purchase price of the motor. For this reason, you will save money from buying better constructed but more expensive motors for high usage equipment.

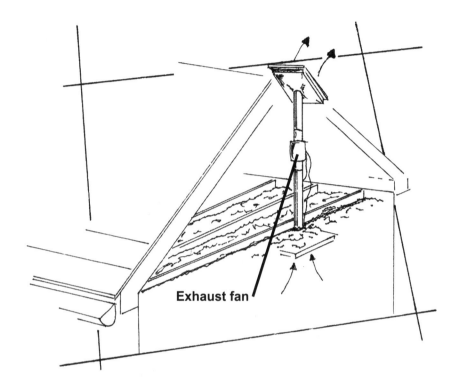

Exhaust fan

HS-1 Mechanical Ventilation Exhaust Fan

Exhaust-Only Ventilation

Exhaust-only systems have all the drawbacks of a balanced system and also do not work very well in airtight houses. They struggle to draw air in through air pathways from the outside to replace air they exhausted out of the house. In addition, any air they do draw in through air pathways comes with hitchhikers such as dust, insulation particles or radon; if you wanted fresh air, you will most likely not get it from this source.

Exhaust-only ventilation fans will also need to compete with other exhaust fans in your house. For example, an average clothes dryer will exhaust approximately 200 cubic feet per minute of air out of your house while you have it running. That is four times the per minute recommended amount of air pulled out of your house for a family of four in a 2000 square foot house. If you do two loads of laundry a day and run your clothes dryer for 45 minutes per each load, you will evacuate 37,500 cubic feet of air out of your house in an hour and half if you include the exhaust-only fan. That is a lot of air to replace and recondition.

You will have a similar effect with range hood fans, bathroom vent fans or combustion appliance power-vented fans. As a matter of fact, exhaust fans can cause backdrafting of atmospherically vented combustion appliances. You will also find that your exhaust fan will need to exhaust more air out of your house during mild spring and fall days and exhaust less during cold winter days. If you have a constant speed fan, you might pull more air out of your house in winter then you need, causing your conditioning system to work harder, which will raise your utility bills. Finally, you will want to make sure that any exhaust fan you have exiting out of your roof is located far away from your soffits, so humid air does not migrate into your attic via your soffits and cause moisture damage or a mold issue.

Supply-Only Ventilation

Supply-only systems ventilate better in cold climates when you have low temperatures outside and warm buoyant air inside. The warm buoyant air pushes on interior boundaries of your house to force interior air through air pathways. As the warm air passes through air pathways, the colder air on the outside will condense moisture from the inside air into your house's building materials and potentially cause moisture damage or mold. In warmer climates where you have less temperature difference between outside and inside, you will not have as much air forced out of your house and you will not get as much air exchange. You also want to make sure you do not have a fresh air intake located close to sources of carbon monoxide or other contaminates to include combustion appliance exhaust ports from your house.

Given the complexity of deciding which ventilation system would work best for your unique conditions, you should contact a Home Energy Rater to provide expert analysis and advice. For example, you might even be able to use a bathroom vent fan as an exhaust system if it exchanges the recommended amount of air and if you can stand the noise from the constantly running fan.

Ventilation System Extras

Heat Recovery Ventilators
You could enhance a mechanical ventilation system with extra performance oriented systems. If you live in a cold climate you might want to install a heat recovery ventilator (HRV). HRVs are a balanced ventilation system that draws fresh air in from the outside and tempers it with your conditioned exhaust air, so the HRV recovers some of the heat from your inside air before it vents it out of your house. These systems tend to work very well and can save you money if you live where it stays cold for long periods of time.

Energy Recovery Ventilators
For additional energy savings, you could install an energy recovery ventilator (ERV), which works like a heat recovery ventilator except that it also acts to conserve humidity levels within your home. In winter, an ERV will not dry out your house as quickly as an HRV. In summer an ERV will limit the amount of humidity brought into a house. This sounds like a better system, but the incremental cost of an ERV compared to an HRV is easier to justify in a hot humid climate.

When deciding if you want to install either an ERV or HRV, you should consider the installation cost, the energy saving capacity of either unit over its service life and the cost saving benefits based on current and estimated future energy prices.

HEPA Filters

If you are prone to allergies or if you live in an area that has low outdoor air quality, such as areas next to major roads, you might want to consider having a HEPA air filtration system installed with your mechanical ventilation system. HEPA filters filter outdoor air as it comes into your house so you get fresh, clean air replacing polluted or stale air in your house. Both HRVs and ERVs can come with a HEPA filter attached, or, if you choose, you can have a HEPA air filter system installed by itself with your ventilation system. You should keep in mind, that due to the high air pressure required to move air through a HEPA filter, operational costs of the HEPA filter may become an issue for you.

The extras you may or may not choose for your house depends on your particular situation. Whatever your situation, I highly recommend you at least have a whole-house mechanical ventilation system rated to the ASHRAE standard. If you have an airtight house built, add it to the builder's list. If you own an airtight house without one, add it to your home improvement project's list. You will breath easier just having it there!

Mold has become the bane of modern construction; so much so that many home-insurance companies have excluded it from their coverage. Stories such as mold taking over houses and people fleeing for their lives have filled builders with liability concern and homeowners with fear for safety of their families along with the resale value of their homes. Given all this commotion you may wonder if you have mold in your house. Well the answer is yes, you do; mold exists in every house because mold is an essential part of the world's ecological system. It is the agent that decomposes all organic material like wood, paper and many other materials which builders use to construct houses. Although your house has mold spores, they need the right conditions in order to thrive. Mold requires a food source, the right temperature and moisture in order to grow into catastrophic proportions that put insurance and homebuilding companies out of business and drive homeowners from their homes.

If you have out of control mold in your house, please treat it like a fire and have it taken care of immediately! Mold literally grows overnight and it can spread from a very small area to a very large area in a short amount of time. Additionally, if you do not know what to do to remove mold, then get someone who does; mold can harm those who do not properly equip themselves to remove it[10]. Finally, when dealing with a mold problem, ensure you identify and rectify the source of moisture that caused the mold. Of the three factors mold needs to thrive, we can only control moisture. Cellulose-based building materials provide an abundant food source for mold and mold thrives at the temperatures we find comfortable. This is why if you have a mold problem, then you also have a moisture problem in your house. If you do not correct the moisture problem the mold will return.

If you believe an ounce of prevention is worth a pound of cure, you should manage moisture inside and outside of your house before mold starts causing problems. In other words, make sure moisture and bulk water outside your house stays outside and excess moisture inside your house ends up outside as well.

Moisture outside your house comes in two varieties: air and ground. Air sources of moisture include rain, frost, ice, snow, fog and humidity and can potentially gain access to your house from your roof tip down to the ground. Ground sources of moisture include any type of moisture that enters your house through its foundation. I will extensively cover ground sources of moisture, and how to keep it out of your house; in chapter seven: Musty Cellars.

Of the three sources of moisture, you will have the most complicated time managing air sources since every house has numerous and unique ways for water to enter. Water vapor gains access to your interior via air pathways; to prevent this, vapor retarders like housewrap and air sealing techniques as discussed in chapter one, Frigid Lair, should take on a whole new importance. You should have a leak free house if you diligently guard against wind driven rain and pursue every location on the exterior of your house that poses an obstacle to a raindrop's path to the ground.

Air Sources of Moisture

Roof Drainage

Your house has many water vulnerable areas, which I have depicted in illustration M-1, pg 78. Luckily, you can inspect and correct these vulnerable areas without tearing apart your house. Anytime water can converge or go vertical to get behind a building material on the exterior of your house you potentially have a problem, which is exactly what makes these areas vulnerable. For example, water converges in roof valleys and potentially backs up and finds a way around shingles and roofing felt to get into your house, or water flowing down your exterior wall converges on a garage roof, porch roof or bay window awning to do the same thing. Wind hitting your roof or the side of your house can drive rain at least 2 inches in a vertical direction. To counter this, your ridge vent should have an extra flange or moisture barrier that blocks wind driven rain or snow from coming up your roof and entering your attic. To stop wind driven rain from pushing water up behind your cladding, any flashing you have should extend at least two and half inches up past the cladding lip that covers it so wind driven rain cannot jump over the top of the flashing.

Crickets

Water can gain access into your attic along the up-slope side of your chimney. Water flowing down your roof into your chimney's upper side does not drain away because the connection between your roof and chimney provides a slope-less trough in which water can sit. Eventually, water will find a way into your attic along this slope-less trough and cause water damage and potentially mold in your attic or ceiling. Roofers should install crickets to prevent this from happening. A cricket looks like a doghouse roof installed between the up-slope side of your chimney and the roof of your house (Illustration M-1a, pg 79). Crickets redirect rainwater to either side of the chimney so water cannot pool along the up-roof side of the chimney and gain access to your house.

Roof Valley

Water converging from your roof can get around your shingles, metal valley flashing and roofing felt in your valley if your roofer did not install them correctly. Prior to installing roofing felt horizontally across your roof your roofer should install roofing felt running the length of the valley. A best practice would be for the roofer to apply peel and stick Ice and Water Shield® in the valley instead of roofing felt. Both methods will direct water that gets under shingles to shed down the valley and into the gutter, but Ice and Water Shield® does a better job then roofing felt.

Roofers should overlap the ends of horizontally run roofing felt on top of the valley roofing felt or Ice and Water Shield® (Illustration M-1b, pg 80). Many roofers weave shingles in a valley without even using flashing. This will not stop water from eventually penetrating your roof and causing water damage to your ceilings. To prevent this, roofers should flash valleys with metal flashing, overlap shingles on it and trim the shingles on either side of the valley to provide a straight uniform appearance.

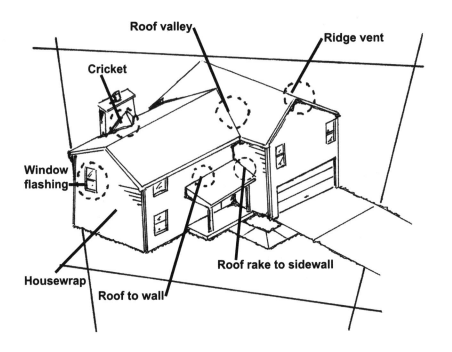

M-1 Water Vulnerable Areas

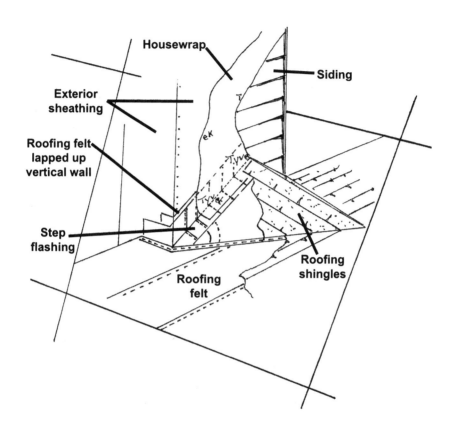

M-1a Cricket

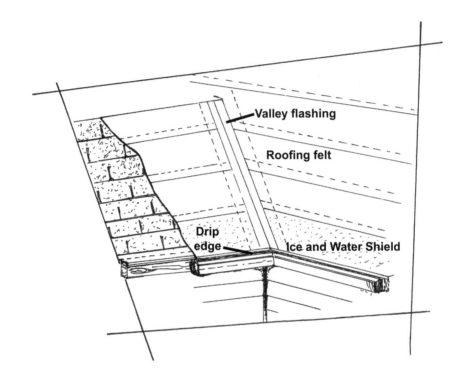

M-1b Roof Valley

Ridge Vent

Ridge vents are vents that run the length of your roofline to allow moisture from your attic to escape. They work in conjunction with your soffit vents. Air enters through the soffit vents and runs up along the bottom of the roof and exits through the ridge vent. This is the best roof ventilation strategy you can have because air runs over the entire underside of the roof. In wind driven rain or snow, raindrops or snowflakes can enter the ridge vent and fall onto your insulation, potentially causing leaks through your ceiling or mold growth in your attic. To prevent this, your ridge vent should have a flange or a moisture barrier that blocks rain and snow from blowing up your roof and into the vent. The flange or moisture barrier will prevent rain and snow from going in but will allow attic air to get out (Illustration M-1c, pg 83).

Roof Rake to Sidewall

Roof to sidewall transitions are most commonly seen where a garage roof attaches to a house. Water coming down the roof will flow against the sidewall, and if your roofer did not properly integrate the different roofing layers, flashing and housewrap, water will get into the interior wall. Water can also enter your house via a roof to sidewall transition through natural fiber siding on your house. Capillary action can cause a cut fiber siding edge to wick water out of the flashing trough and release it where it has an opportunity to get inside your house.

To thwart both of these potential moisture damage causing defects, you should ensure your roofer first laps the roofing felt from the roof up the sidewall, then integrates sheet metal step flashing with each row of shingles. He should install step flashing so it will extend at least two and half inches up past the cut line of your exterior cladding on the sidewall. If using housewrap, he should lap it over the step flashing; if not, he should apply an adhesive membrane strip on the step flashing's top edge so part of it covers the flashing and the other part is taped to the sidewall above.

To prevent capillary action from occurring at the cut edge of your cladding, you should have at least one and half-inches of flashing showing from the roof to the beginning of the cut line of your cladding (Illustration M-1d, pg 84). For brick cladding, roofers need to cut into the mortar joint to attach step flashing for each row of shingles. All of which sounds very complicated but is also very logical if observed from the aspect of a raindrop rolling down the outside of your house trying to gain entry in any way possible; including wind blowing it up and over a flashing lip. Take some time to study illustration M-1d and you should start to understand raindrop logic.

Kickout Flashing
Water flowing down the flashing of your roof to sidewall transition will either overwhelm the corner of your house's main wall or overwhelm the wall itself if you do not have it redirected to a gutter. The overwhelmed corner or wall will deteriorate and allow more water into your house over time which can lead to interior water damage and mold. Kickout flashing redirects this water away from your house's corner or wall so water flows down the gutter instead of into your house (Illustration M-1d, pg 84).

Roof to Wall
Roof to wall transitions are very similar to roof rake to sidewall transitions. You will want to make sure your roofer integrates the different roofing layers, flashing and housewrap in the same manner as described above. The only difference this time is that instead of individual step flashing the roofer should use L-flashing. Just like above, you want to make sure your flashing extends at least two and half inches above your siding's bottom piece and you have at least an inch and half gap between the bottom of the flashing and your siding's bottom piece (Illustration M-1e, pg 85).

Roof Eave
In snow prone cold climates you will want your roofer to install a drip edge and Ice and Water Shield® on and over your roof eaves to guard against potential ice damming. When snow accumulates on your roof the sun will melt it and melted snow will drain towards the gutter. On many roofs, eaves tend to be colder than the rest of the roof so when melted snow runs across this portion of the roof it re-freezes causing an ice dam. Soffit vents and roof ridge vents help prevent this by allowing air from

outside to flow underneath the entire surface of the roof and out the ridge vent, which tends to keep the entire roof at the same temperature.

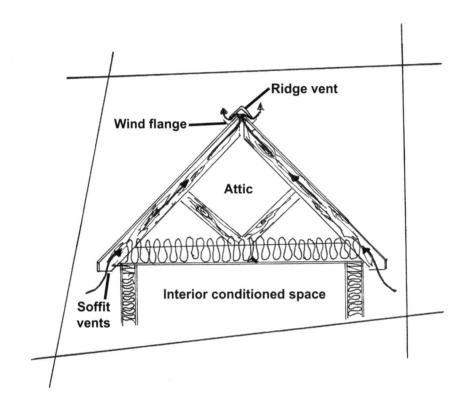

M-1c Ridge Vent

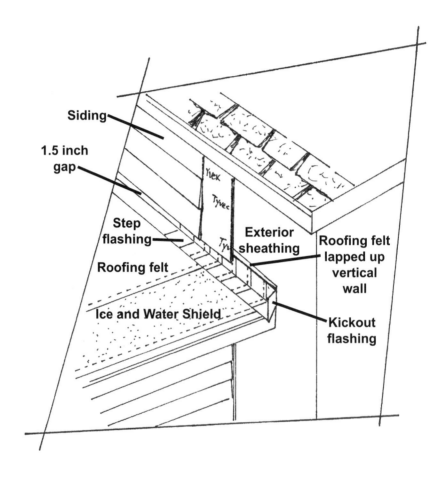

Siding

1.5 inch gap

Step flashing

Roofing felt

Ice and Water Shield

Exterior sheathing

Roofing felt lapped up vertical wall

Kickout flashing

M-1d Roof Rake to Sidewall

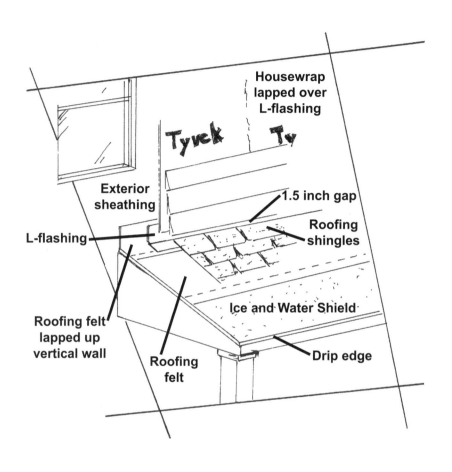

Housewrap
lapped over
L-flashing

Tyvek   Ty

Exterior
sheathing

1.5 inch gap

Roofing
shingles

L-flashing

Roofing felt
lapped up
vertical wall

Ice and Water Shield

Roofing
felt

Drip edge

M-1e Roof to Wall

If this does not work you will want to have a drip edge and Ice and Water Shield® applied at your eaves so water from ice dams does not penetrate through shingles and roofing felt to waterlog and eventually rot your roof eaves. A drip edge is an L-shaped piece of flashing builders install on roof edges to direct water into the gutter, away from the fascia and from being forced back up under roofing materials. Ice and Water Shield® is a rubber-like membrane that sheds water better than other building materials, so when used at roof eaves water will have a more difficult time penetrating through it into your attic (Illustration M-1e, pg 85).

Gutters and Gutter Down-Spouts
Gutters provide an important function in collecting large volumes of water flowing down your roof surfaces in a rain storm and directing it out and away from your house's foundation. If you do not have gutters or some other method for directing roof water away from your foundation and you live in a rain prone climate, you might want to have them installed. If you have gutters, they will not do you any good if your gutter down-spouts terminate next to your foundation or, even worse, someone has connected them into your foundation drainage system that runs beside your footer. Either method can cause you to have a basement or crawlspace moisture issue or, in extreme cases, basement or crawlspace flooding. Even if you have a slab-on-grade house built, you should have your gutter down-spouts terminate at least 6 feet from your foundation and have water drain in a downhill direction away from your foundation wall.

Drainage Plane
Your house wall's main line of defense for shedding bulk water from outside is its drainage plane. The drainage plane is the surface underneath your house's brick, vinyl, stone, stucco or other cladding system and it sheds bulk water down to the bottom and away from the interior of your house (Illustration M-1f, pg 91). The drainage plane must shed water to the outside because moisture will get behind any type of cladding you have. Most builders use housewrap as the drainage plane because housewrap acts like a more moisture permeable Gortex® raincoat for your house. It is moisture permeable because you do not want moisture coming out from the inside of your house and becoming trapped behind housewrap.

Housewrap works by shedding bulk water but also allows moisture vapor to pass through it. This keeps most water out but allows your exterior wall to dry if bulk water or moisture vapor should enter it. Accordingly, you can think of housewrap this way: we wear raincoats over our skin and houses wear them under theirs.

In order for housewrap to work properly, builders must overlap it shingle style (Illustration M-1g, pg 92), going up the side of the house with the horizontal and vertical seams taped. This keeps water flowing down it to the outside as it passes to each new sheet of housewrap. For houses using foam sheathing or other non-housewrap material for their drainage plane, ensure your builder tapes all vertical and horizontal seams with manufacturer approved tape for the type of drainage plane material used. To make the drainage plane complete, builders must integrate windows and doors into it, so water sheds to the outside around them as well. From a statistical standpoint, window water leakage is usually the biggest water management problem in houses.

If a builder did not install a drainage plane during construction or he did it incorrectly, you will find it very expensive to rectify. A notable exception to his is if you are planning to have your cladding replaced, you should also plan to have your drainage plane inspected and, if necessary, corrected or installed at the same time.

Window Flashing
Windows come with flanges that installers use to attach to the exterior of houses. Unfortunately, these flanges also can catch water flowing down a house's drainage plane. For this reason, builders must integrate these flanges with drainage planes so water flows to the outside instead of into a house. Depending on drainage plane material, the detail can change, but in general the technique stays the same. If using housewrap, builders should apply it on the house, cut out the window opening and cut a flap over the window opening. Next, they should install a Peel & Stick™ flexible membrane wrap on the bottom of the rough window opening, which overlaps the outside edge at least six inches and continues up both sides of the rough opening at least three inches. They should then apply caulk on the sides and top around the window opening where the flanges

attach but do not caulk the bottom edge. After caulking, they should install the window with flanges over the drainage plane material on the sides and bottom and cover the top flange with the housewrap flap. Finally, they should apply tape-type flashing on the sides and top over the flanges (Illustration M-1h, pg 93). For houses without housewrap, builders or window installers take all the same steps except for those involving housewrap.

Weep Holes

As explained above, bulk water will get behind any type of cladding you have on your house. Brick or stone walls pose a greater risk of this because in sunny weather, the sun will drive moisture in brick and stone towards the interior side of the cladding wall. Even without solar drive in wind driven rain, a twelve square foot section of brick cladding can leak a gallon to a gallon and half of water per hour. This adds up to a lot of water behind your cladding that needs someplace to go other than into your house. To alleviate this, you should ensure your builder installs weep holes every 4 feet at the base of your brick cladding. They should also install weep holes over window, door and garage door ledges. Weep holes are gaps between bricks without any mortar applied between them so that bulk water can drain out from behind the wall. Brick cladding with weep holes sometimes gets clogged from excess mortar that falls down between the house and brick cladding. To prevent this, your builder should install a mortar catch screen at the bottom of your wall between your house's drainage plane and your brick cladding. The mortar catch screen will catch mortar droppings so they do not clog weep holes. Finally, to better help your wall to dry, you should have air holes installed at the top of the brick cladding. The air holes, installed just like weep holes but at the top, allow air to enter at the top and exit through weep holes at the bottom, taking moisture vapor with it.

Stucco Weep Screeds

Stucco coated walls experience an issue similar to brick walls in that they need an area at the bottom of the stucco to allow moisture to drain out and away from your house. You can accomplish this with a weep screed. Weep screeds come in a variety of designs; all of them provide a perforated flange that acts as a bottom boundary for your stucco coating where the perforations allow moisture to drain past the screed. When inspecting your weep screed, you need to make sure you have at least 4 inches between your weep screed and your finished ground surface. If you have concrete walkways or some other hard surface installed up to your house's foundation, you should ensure you have at least 2 inches between the weep screed and the hard surface. Finally, you should make sure neither you nor anyone else covers your weep screeds with landscaping or concrete walkways.

Interior Sources of Moisture

Interior sources of moisture are less problematic but require your management to keep them in check. They become problematic when moisture tries to go through your exterior walls to the outside but gets trapped and turns to liquid. The steady accumulation of this liquid over time enables mold spores in your walls to activate and spread over a large area. You can prevent this by keeping humidity levels in your house between 0% and 65%[11].

To control humidity levels in your house, you need to rid your house of excess moisture caused mainly by cooking and showering. That is why you should have exhaust fans vented to the outside in kitchens and bathrooms and use them regularly. For example, boiling water on your stove concentrates moisture-laden air in one area, which can lead to a mold problem. So, make sure you vent the steam out of your house when you cook. Be advised, if you have a re-circulating range hood fan, you are only drawing moisture-laden air from your stove top and blowing it back into your kitchen. To avoid this situation, ensure your range hood fan vents to the outside so you can keep steam from your pot of spaghetti from becoming a kitchen mold problem. It is better to have an ugly vent installed in your house than to have an ugly mold problem in your walls.

Your bathroom, like your kitchen, can deliver an equivalent amount of moisture in a concentrated area especially when you have many people taking showers everyday. Again, you should run your bathroom exhaust fan anytime someone takes a shower. So that you will not have to worry about you or your family members remembering to do it regularly, you might want to install a fan with a humidistat. The humidistat would turn your fan on when humidity in your bathroom reaches a predetermined level and keep it on until the humidity gets back down to your set level.

Some bathrooms do not have vent fans because certain local building codes do not require bathrooms with a window to the outside to have them. I find this amusing since most people will not open their bathroom window in the dead of winter to let out excess moisture. Besides, even if you did open your window in winter, you do not have any assurances whether air will move in or out of the window. If you have a bathroom with a tub or shower and without an exhaust fan, you should have an exhaust fan installed and use it. As a further precaution against potential mold, make sure the fan actually vents to the outside instead of terminating in your attic. Vent fans that terminate in attics provide moisture needed to have an attic mold problem.

You can live worry free about mold if you successfully manage moisture in and around your house. Each house has its nuances, yet moisture and water always behave in the same manner; so think about a raindrop and moisture vapor in each situation you encounter and work to keep excessive moisture out of your house.

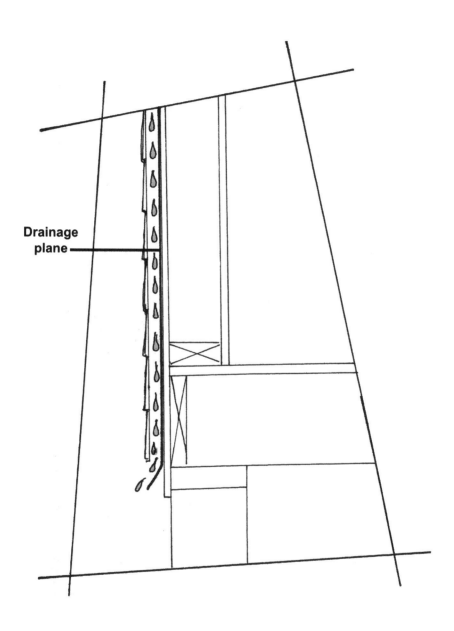

Drainage plane

M-1f Drainage Plane

Housewrap overlapped shingle style

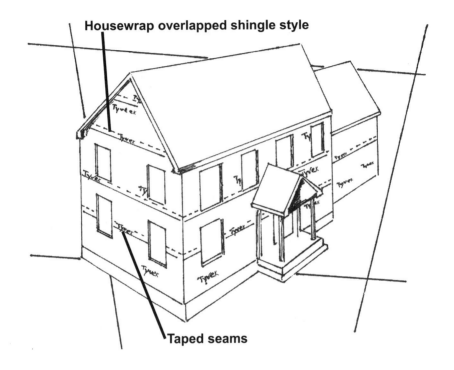

Taped seams

M-1g Drainage Plane Installation

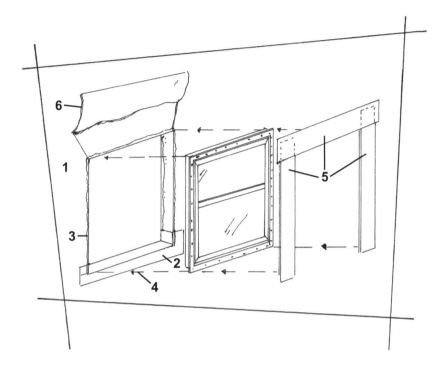

M-1h Window Flashing

1. Apply housewrap over wall and cut flap above window opening.
2. Apply sill flashing on sill.
3. Caulk opening around window.
4. Install window.
5. Apply flashing to the jams and head overlapping window flanges and housewrap.
6. Bring flap down over head flashing and tape cuts.

I loved our basement while growing up, it was where my siblings and I could go to run and play without messing up the more formal rooms of my parents' house or breaking family heirlooms. I loved it so much I didn't notice the cold clammy musty smell that came along with it but I do remember painting the walls many times with so called waterproof paint in an effort to keep moisture out which never seemed to work as expected. Consequently, things we stored down there became so moldy over time that we had to throw much of them away.

You may have similar experiences with your current basement, or you may have temporarily stopped moisture with waterproof paint only to have it overwhelmed by the next big rain. When you build below the surface of the ground, you are fighting some powerful forces of nature, which literally push and wick moisture into and through your foundation walls and floors.

Hydrostatic Pressure
When water enters the soil it doesn't just drain away, hydrostatic pressure also pushes it through the soil. In bodies of water, hydrostatic pressure is the force that keeps ships afloat. Imagine the force that keeps an aircraft carrier from sinking, pushing against your house's porous foundation walls.

Capillary Action
In conjunction with hydrostatic pressure, concrete and cinder block will wick moisture like a tree root and deliver it inside your house via capillary action. In houses, nature tries to keep everything in balance by taking moisture from the ground and transferring it to relatively moisture free basements. You have hydrostatic pressure keeping foundation floors and walls stocked with moisture from the ground while capillary action wicks it through and into the house. Unprotected, basement floors and foundation walls do not stand a chance of keeping moisture out.

Foundation Drainage System

You should not have any moisture problems in your basement if you have a drainage system that diverts water away from your foundation walls and floor. Your drainage system should consist of a perforated foundation drain pipe on either side of your footer to move water away from your house, a drainage plane around your foundation walls to redirect hydrostatically delivered water to the perforated foundation drain pipe, and a capillary break to prevent moisture from coming through your basement floor (Illustration MC-1, pg 97). If your basement slab is below the invert level of the municipal storm water piping, you will need to use a sump pit and a sump pump to keep water out. To prevent burrowing rodents from entering the drainage system, any drains that open to daylight should have a louvered cap on the termination. Chipmunks and ground squirrels find these systems to be excellent homes except for the lack of a back door, which they will make themselves by enlarging a pipe perforation and tunneling to the surface, filling the pipe with dirt in their wake.

Foundation Drains

Foundation drains work best if you have them placed as low to the bottom of your footer as structurally possible so it will keep any bulk water that accumulates down there away from your footer. To help water drain to the drain pipe you should bury the drain pipe under at least 3 feet of crushed gravel. Over time, fine silt will clog crushed gravel so you also need to wrap the gravel with a silt screen that allows water to flow through while keeping fine silt back.

Foundation Drainage Planes

Underground drainage planes only work if they counteract hydrostatic forces; to do this they must hold back soil while allowing water to flow through. You can accomplish this by covering your foundation wall with some kind of silt screen over a highly water resistant grooved surface like closed cell foam or a plastic, spongy fiber-like material, like Enkadrain®, which allows moisture to pass but keeps soil back. You can find both of these types of products on the market and for easy reference I have them listed in appendix D.

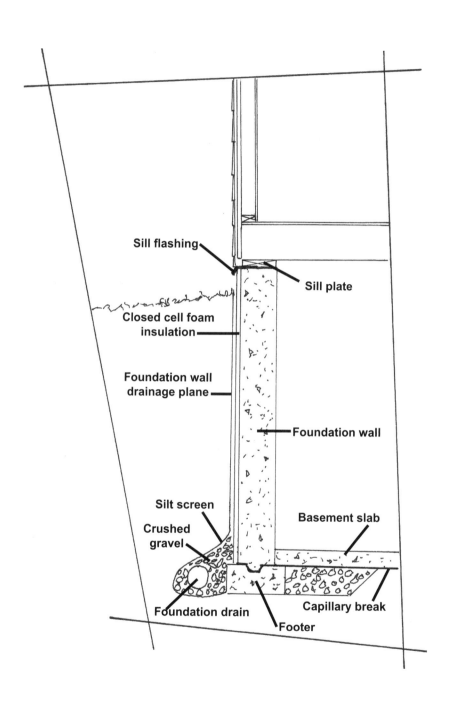

MC-1 Foundation Drainage System

Either way; this type of material needs to completely cover the exterior of your foundation walls so moisture flows down to the drain pipe and out and away from your house. Insulated drainage plane material provides an added bonus for your walls. Keeping your foundation walls warm from the outside enables much more comfort for you on the inside.

This drainage system may seem unlikely for you to install if you already own a house. Yet, we moved into a house that had a severe moisture problem in our basement. As part of the closing agreement the seller agreed to fix the moisture problem. The previous owners hired a local company to come in, jackhammer the interior perimeter of our basement and install a drain pipe on the interior side of the footer. After its installation, moisture still came through our foundation wall into our basement, so except for installing a capillary-break under the slab, I took it upon myself to install a functional drainage system.

I had our house's foundation excavated down to the footer and I did the rest of the work myself including buying all materials. All totaled, not including the cost of my labor, it cost less than it did to have a new roof installed on our house. After I installed the drainage system, we had heavy rains which caused local flooding, and many of our neighbors had to throw away carpets and redo sections of their basements from water damage caused by the overwhelming rain water getting into their basements. As proof that this system works, our basement, which sits lower than theirs, stayed completely dry. The drainage system worked as designed and the exterior insulation has also made our basement warmer in winter.

Stopping Capillary Action
You also need to stop moisture from entering your basement from your foundation slab floor and footer. You can accomplish this by using a capillary-break, which works similar to a firebreak in that it does not allow moisture to pass from one side to the other. 6mm plastic sheets applied underneath your basement floor and footer makes a great capillary-break. The 6mm plastic will stop moisture from coming into contact with your basement floor and footer to

thwart the forces of capillary action. You can also install plastic sheets between the footer and the foundation wall instead of putting it underneath the footer, but you need to ensure you have your foundation wall anchored to the footer via rebar. Like other techniques I have explained, you can only accomplish any of this before you have your footers and basement floor poured. If you already live in your house or are buying an existing house, you are out of luck, just as we were in all of our houses.

Even if you do not have a basement in your house, you can still apply these techniques since every house has a foundation. Insulating and keeping water away from your foundation makes good sense for every house. By doing so, you will be more comfortable in your house and have fewer maintenance issues. When it comes to moisture damage on our house, I would rather spend money up front and not have a problem instead of worrying about mold growth afterwards.

None of us ever think we could inadvertently turn our house into a hazardous gas chamber; yet that is exactly what could happen when we do not take carbon monoxide as seriously as we should.

Carbon monoxide is a poisonous, colorless, odorless and tasteless gas produced from incomplete burning of carbon-containing fuels such as natural gas and propane. Nearly 300 people die each year from carbon monoxide exposure related to household combustion appliances and thousands of others become ill or suffer permanent effects from carbon monoxide poisoning.

Carbon monoxide binds to hemoglobin in your blood, which reduces your blood's ability to carry oxygen, and deprives your brain, heart and other vital organs of the oxygen they need. This, for example, could cause you to lose concentration, retard growth of your brain, or exacerbate a heart condition. It can also cause lasting health harm through destructive effects on your central nervous system.

You will find it hard to diagnose carbon monoxide poisoning because you can easily confuse the symptoms with other illnesses; the most common signs are headaches, dizziness, weakness, nausea, vomiting, chest pain, and confusion. Sleeping or intoxicated people can even die from carbon monoxide poisoning before ever experiencing symptoms.

Each of us has a different tolerance to carbon monoxide poisoning, but unborn babies, infants, young and elderly people, and people with anemia or a history of heart or respiratory disease are most at risk. Pets are even susceptible to carbon monoxide poisoning.

Carbon monoxide can build up in enclosed or semi-enclosed spaces such that it forms pockets of concentrated carbon monoxide. For example, air surrounding a carbon monoxide detector may read acceptable, but a few feet away you might have an unacceptably high concentration of carbon monoxide.

Hopefully now, you better understand the seriousness of carbon monoxide poisoning; so allow me to help you understand how it could get into your house. Carbon monoxide can enter your house from a variety of sources; the three main gas appliance culprits: gas stoves, gas furnaces and gas water heaters can work well if you have safer models installed and use them appropriately.

Anytime you burn gas or other fossil fuels, the combustion process releases carbon monoxide into the air. Ideally, you should never allow carbon monoxide to come in contact with your house's breathable air. Instead, you should have appliances, which manufacturers make, with totally enclosed and separate flue systems dedicated to venting carbon monoxide out of your house.

Gas Appliances

Gas Stoves
You cannot have a totally enclosed and separate system to vent gas stove carbon monoxide out because you use the direct flame to heat your food. For this reason, you should turn on your range hood fan prior to lighting the stove and only turn it off after you turn off the stove. If you have a re-circulating fan instead of a fan that vents to the outside, then you have a problem. Re-circulating fans draw air from the range top and blow it back into your kitchen, so if you are trying to get carbon monoxide out of your house, your re-circulating range hood fan will not do it for you. If you prefer cooking with gas stoves, please make sure you have a range hood fan with a flue to the outside and use it every time you cook.

Atmospherically Vented Water Heaters
Atmospherically vented water heaters pose a less commonly identified, but more serious threat than other household combustion appliances. You can identify atmospherically vented gas water heaters by the open flues on top of the water tank. When operating properly, gas burns below the water tank, which heats the water, and the exhaust naturally rises up the outside of the tank to a tube in the center, then to the flue and finally outside your house (Illustration GC-1, 103). When backdrafting occurs, air from outside comes down the water tank flue and exhaust goes in your house

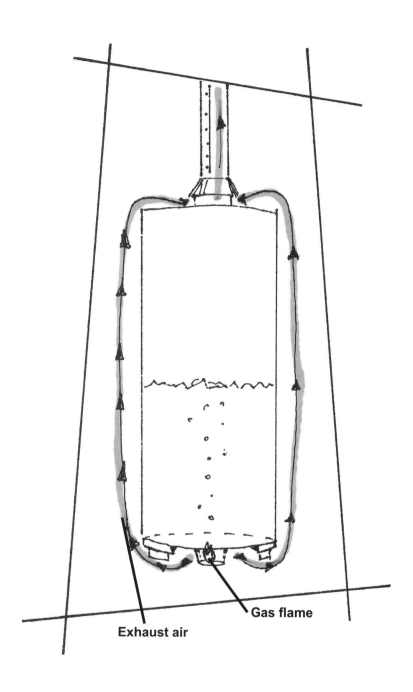

Gas flame

Exhaust air

GC-1 Atmospherically Vented Water Heater

instead of up the flue. Your water tank flue can backdraft frequently due to pressure imbalances in your house potentially caused by one or a combination of the following: central air system, large kitchen range hood fans, open-hearth fireplaces, clothes dryers and other types of exhaust fans. When your water tank flue backdrafts, you get carbon monoxide delivered into your house instead of going outside. For example, when not enough air gets back to your air handler it draws replacement air from the closest source, which often happens to be the open flue at the top of your water heater. Your air handler will most likely distribute the carbon monoxide throughout your house via your air ducts. Since this option should not appeal to you, and if you still prefer using gas appliances, I highly recommend you use either sealed combustion or power-vented appliances.

Sealed Combustion and Power-Vented Gas Appliances

Both sealed combustion and power-vented gas appliances work well. Between the two, sealed combustion appliances are the better choice. They have a totally enclosed flue system that keeps carbon monoxide from the rest of your house; so carbon monoxide has no other place to go other than up and out of your house.

Power-vented gas appliances are in some cases an acceptable second choice. They have a fan blowing up the flue so the flue will more likely act like a flue instead of an air intake. Power-vented gas appliance have drawbacks which include: they cannot share a common flue with atmospherically vented equipment, and in an airtight house they cause pressure imbalances that also cause backdrafting of other atmospherically vented gas appliances. You can easily install both of these systems as a new item or to replace an existing system. Replacing them will not save you any money, but they may save your life or the lives of loved ones.

Other Potential Sources of Carbon Monoxide

Other potential sources of carbon monoxide in your house include your garage and ventless gas fireplaces. Garages most often become a source of carbon monoxide when you park your car or cars in them. Cars will produce more carbon monoxide at start up than they do after they have warmed up, but even so cars will continue to release carbon monoxide for up to 30 minutes after you turn off their ignition. You should minimize the time a car runs in your garage by not warming it up there and by shutting it off immediately after you pull in. To ensure carbon monoxide in your garage stays out of your house, you should also investigate air pathways between your house and an attached or integral garage.

Attached and Integral Garages

Attached garages share a common wall with your house, whereas integral garages take up space within your house. Both attached and integral garages might exchange air with the rest of your house, and if they do, carbon monoxide from your car *will* get into your house.

Attached garages will exchange air both through holes in your garage/house common wall and around the door that goes between your house and your garage. This happens for the same reason your rooms get cold, because builders may not have insulated and air sealed your common wall or installed an exterior-grade door between your garage and your house.

For attached garages, you should treat the common wall between your garage and your house as an exterior wall and have it insulated and air sealed appropriately. In addition, make sure you have an air tight exterior grade door between your house and your garage. For heated attached garages, insulating the common wall is not as important, but air sealing it is very important in order to keep carbon monoxide out.

Integral garages are even more difficult to isolate from the rest of your house for many reasons, but mostly due to floor joists supporting the floor above. The floor joists provide big air duct-like tunnels for air to transfer between your garage and the rest of your house. The best way to stop this air exchange is to have commercially applied foam insulation sprayed into your garage joist bays and then further seal them off by gluing and screwing 5/8-inch sheets of drywall to the bottom of your floor joists. You could also remove a 16-inch width of ceiling plaster along the wall adjacent to the rest of your house so you could blow in cellulose and put blocking between joists. If neither of these methods appeal to you then you could accomplish the same effect in many other ways, just remember your objective is to insulate and air seal your integral garage from the rest of your house. Some integral garages have attic spaces above them, so in this case make sure you seal them off by gluing and screwing 5/8-inch sheets of drywall to the bottom of your roof trusses. You will also need to treat the wall(s) and door between your house and garage like an exterior wall and door to keep air from transferring in those locations. Finally, you might want to install a low power fan electrically connected to your garage door to draw air out of your garage. You electrically connect the fan to the garage door so it comes on when you open and close your garage door and have it set to stay on for as long as it takes to pull out residual carbon monoxide or for at least 30 minutes at a time. The fan will pull air from your house, through any un-sealed air pathways, into your garage and then outside, instead of the other way around.

Air Ducts in Garage

For those of you with an air handler or air ducts in your garage, you are just asking to have your garage's air spread to the four corners of your house. As I mentioned before, air ducts leak, and although you can decrease the amount they leak you can never stop them from leaking. If you have an air handler or air ducts in your garage you should try to relocate them to a place within your house or at least isolate them from the air in your garage. Remember, your central air system works better when you have its air ducts within conditioned spaces of your house, so if you can't move them to conditioned spaces, then bring conditioned spaces to them. In other words, build, insulate and air seal a wall around the air handler and ducts in your garage. As a note, if you do this with an atmospherically vented furnace, you must install a vent to the outside so the air handler will draw make-up air from outside instead of from the garage.

Ventless Gas Fireplaces

Many homeowners have installed ventless gas fireplaces because they can put them anywhere in their homes without the hassle of installing a vent to the outside. By doing so they are creating another carbon monoxide and moisture source without giving themselves the ventilation they should demand. Some gas fireplace manufacturers will tell you they make safe products, while other gas fireplace manufacturers refuse to even produce a ventless variety due to the potential health hazard. Given what you now know about carbon monoxide, why take the risk? Besides, you do not need a chimney to install a vented gas fireplace into your house; the installer can run the vent through most exterior walls. So, don't settle for a ventless gas fireplace, spend the extra money to have a vent system and make sure the vented gas fireplace has sealed tempered glass between you and the fire. This will also help you breath easier!

Carbon monoxide is a very dangerous gas, one which you should not take lightly. Please check your house for sources of carbon monoxide that I have listed and get them corrected if you need to. You will be very happy you did, and if you never have a problem with carbon monoxide, it is one less thing you have to worry about.

Hopefully you have a better understanding of how houses should function and the many reasons they may not function well. You need to remember that every house should do these three things: 1. Stop heat, air and moisture from transferring through its walls, ceilings and foundation, 2. Provide fresh air for its occupants and 3. Control carbon monoxide. If your house does these three things well then you have a Good House! If it does not, and you would like to improve your house's performance, then you should analyze your symptoms, determine the cause and decide if you can cost-effectively fix it or not.

If you have a house built and you would like it to perform to Good House standards you should set performance standards with your builder and specifically address the five types of defects: air pathways, conditioning, insulation, safety, and ventilation, explained in the chapters.

You will have a more comfortable house by eliminating as many insulation, air pathway and conditioning system defects from your house as you cost effectively can. You will have a healthier house by having a properly functioning ventilation system and controlling mold. You will have a safer house if you control carbon monoxide. You will have a more durable house if you control moisture since moisture is the prime ingredient in deteriorating houses. Finally, you will have a more energy efficient house by doing the things that make a house comfortable. Energy efficiency and comfort come as a single package, so you receive double the benefit by trying to achieve one or the other.

Whether you want to improve your house or build one to higher standards, you will find the Quick Reference Guide and the Good House Inspection Checklist very useful. I have organized the Quick Reference Guide alphabetically by the five defect types and the Good House Inspection Checklist by stages of construction. You can use the Quick Reference Guide to help refresh your memory on specific defects and recommended improvements. If you build a house, you can follow the construction process via the Good House Inspection Checklist and inspect what you need during each construction stage; or you could use it on an existing house where applicable.

Whatever you do with your house or one that you plan to buy or build, I hope that you find this book valuable in making decisions about them. Good luck in all your Good House endeavors!

Endnotes

1. For more detailed information about air sealing and insulating this area, refer to Cantilevered Floors in the Framing Chapter of EEBAs Builder's Guide for your climate zone at www.eeba.org.

2. You can reference your local codes at http://global.ihs.com, select the Standards tab and look for International Code Council (ICC) in the dropdown box, or you can call a local building inspector and ask them.

3. For more information on attic insulation refer to www.buildiq.com/ins104.htm.

4. Not only do ducts in exterior walls temper your conditioned air, they also reduce your wall's ability to slow the transfer of heat through that area.

5. You can find out more about AeroSeal® by going to www.aeroseal.com

6. When installing paper-faced fiberglass batts you should put the paper-facing towards where the most moisture comes from. Therefore, in cold climates the paper goes towards the inside of the house, in hot climates it goes towards the exterior of the house.

7. Fiberglass exterior insulation also works very well, although, it will lose some of its R-value when it gets wet, but it will drain moisture away from your crawlspace or foundation wall without anything else added to it.

8. A thin impervious piece of material placed in construction to prevent water penetration or direct the flow of water.

9. ASHRAE Standard 62.2.

10. For more information on mold check www.buildingscience.com under Homeowner Information Resources.

11. ASHRAE Standard 55.

Appendix A
Quick Reference Guide

I have alphabetically arranged each of the five defect types into their own section: Air Pathways, Conditioning, Insulation, Safety and Ventilation. I have further alphabetically arranged the defects within each of the five sections. Each section explains the defects of the topic, inspection check(s) you can make, and what diagnostics, if any, you can have conducted to help validate the performance of the house's system. For simplicity, I have combined health and durability related defects into safety. For added understanding, please keep the goal of each section in mind when referencing the defects in this guide:

Air Pathways: Every house should be as airtight as you can economically achieve.

Conditioning: All houses should have a conditioning system that heats or cools each room to your desired level of comfort without needing auxiliary systems.

Insulation: Every house should have insulation that surrounds it like a space suit, leaving no area on the walls, uppermost ceiling or floor uncovered.

Safety: Every house should effectively control mold and carbon monoxide.

Ventilation: Every house should have a ventilation system that supplies you with fresh air to the ASHRAE standard.

Air Pathways

Band Joists
If not air sealed or insulated, band joists will allow air and heat to pass through the entire perimeter of the house.

Check(s):
Air Sealed Band Joists pg. 28
Where possible, check the interior side of the band joist to ensure the contractors insulated and air sealed the band joist bays. At a minimum, they should at least install fiberglass batts into each bay. Optimally, they should spray foam insulation into this area to both insulate and air seal the band joist bays; otherwise, you will find air sealing the band joist very difficult and time consuming.

Cable and Wire Penetrations
Cable and wire penetrations through the exterior walls, ceiling and floor can admit enough air to significantly alter the temperature of your rooms and cause drafts.

Check(s):
Spray-Foamed Penetrations pg. 27
Check that any cable or wire penetration into the house has spray-foam sealant applied into the hole. Spray-foam will insulate and block the air pathway through the penetration.

Door to Garage
Non-exterior rated doors between the garage and house will allow heat and air to transfer through them.

Check(s):
Exterior Rated Door to Garage pg. 105
Check to ensure that any door leading to a garage from conditioned spaces is an exterior rated door. Exterior rated doors will provide the best air seal and thermal protection of any type of door on the market.

Drywall
In houses with interior drywall, the drywall acts as a barrier to air that makes its way into the stud bays of the house from outside. Therefore, any unsealed cracks, seams or penetrations in the drywall will allow outside air into the house.

Check(s):
Continuous Bead of Glue pg. 25
Check to ensure the contractors have applied a continuous bead of glue that runs on all exterior wall stud surfaces onto which they install drywall. This creates an airtight seal, like a rubber gasket, to reduce the amount of outside air that normally gets in through seams around the drywall.

Outlets and Switch Boxes pg. 7
Check to ensure the builder has either installed outlet and switch boxes with gaskets or have sealed the cable access holes with spray foam on exterior walls.

Foundation Wall Sill Plate
Air will gain access to your house between your foundation wall and the sill plate. Although weather treated, unprotected, your sill plate will absorb moisture from your foundation wall via capillary action.

Check(s):
Foundation Wall Sill Plate Gaskets pg. 28
Foundation wall sill plate gaskets are a foam membrane, wide enough to cover the entire surface of the sill plate, which builders apply between the foundation wall and the wooden sill plate. The gasket will seal this air pathway, as well as stop the moisture transfer between the foundation wall and wooden sill plate.

Leaky Air Ducts
Excessive air duct leakage can significantly decrease comfort of the house and cause house pressure zones. Common causes of air duct leakage include unsealed connections and panned returns.

Check(s):
Air Sealed Ducts pg. 46
Check to ensure ducts have either UL 181 water based mastic or tape on the connection seams. Also, make sure the builder does not install panned supply or return ducts. Alternatively, for

existing houses with leaky ducts, you can apply AeroSeal® in the duct system to help seal them.

Open-Hearth Fireplaces
Open-hearth Fireplaces provide a large air pathway in the house; furthermore, burning a fire in the open-hearth fireplace increases the rate of air flow out of the house.

Check(s):
Direct-Vent Gas Fireplace Inserts pg. 68
Obviously, not having an open-hearth fireplace will completely remedy this defect; however, if you would still like to enjoy the aesthetic appeal of a fire and gain some warmth from it, you should look into direct-vent gas fireplaces. They have aesthetic appeal of an open-hearth fireplace without most of the hassle, mess, drafts or energy loss. Alternatively, wood stoves and open-hearth fireplaces with combustion air drawn directly from the outside can solve a part of the traditional open-hearth fireplace issues.

Garage and House Common Wall
The garage common wall should not exchange heat or air with the rest of the house.

Check(s):
Insulated and Air Sealed Common Wall pg. 105
Check to ensure the builder insulates and air seals the garage common wall as if it is an exterior wall. Insulating and air sealing the wall includes a continuous bead of glue under the bottom plate and on top of the top plate, completely filled stud bays, continuous bead of glue where the drywall edges attach to the wall studs and gasket type or foam sealed outlet and switch boxes. Alternatively, if you own a pre-existing house, you can install a garage-opener-activated exhaust fan in the garage to pull air from the house into the garage instead of the other way around.

Recessed Lights

Recessed lights should not allow air to pass through the light to the other side.

Check(s):
Airtight Recessed Lights pg. 112
Check to ensure you have enclosed recessed lights. Enclosed recessed lights do not have air slits in the top to allow air to pass.

Exterior Wall Bottom and Top Plates

The wood-to-wood connection between the sub-floor and bottom 2x4 or 2x6 of the exterior walls and between the two top plates will not stop air from forcing its way through. This can cause drafts, higher utility bills and reduce house comfort.

Check(s):
Exterior Wall Bottom Plate Seal pg. 28
Check to ensure you have a continuous bead of glue between the top of the sub-floor and bottom of the 2x4 or 2x6 exterior walls.

Exterior Wall Top Plate Seal pg. 28
Check to ensure you have a continuous bead of glue on top of your exterior wall's top plate.

Windows and Doors

A gap between the window or door casing and the house should not allow air to pass.

Check(s):
Foam Insulation in Rough Opening pg. 26
Check to ensure you have foam insulation filling the gap between the window or door casing and the house. In some cases the gap may be to small to foam, in which case you should caulk it.

Air Pathways Tests

Blower Door Tests provide results that indicate how well the house is air sealed. Home Energy Raters conduct a test by attaching a fan in the doorway and turning it on to pressurize the house. Once the fan establishes a pre-determined pressure in the house, instruments attached to the fan indicate how many cubic feet per minute (cfm) of air the house needs to maintain pressure. The cfm is the leakage rate of the house and it is given in units of air changes per hour (ACH). Using results from this device, a well air sealed house will have less than 4 ACH; a very well air sealed house will have less than 2 ACH and anything less than 1 ACH is fantastic.

Conditioning

Air Duct Sizing

An HVAC contractor must have all ducts in the house appropriately designed and installed to provide calculated room-to-room target air flow.

Check(s):
Duct Layout Floor Plan pg. 40
Check for a floor plan showing the target air flow for each room, duct sizes, types of duct fittings (elbows, bends, i.e., anything other than a straight piece of duct), and the equivalent length for each duct run.

Air Ducts

Excessive air duct leakage can significantly decrease comfort of the house and cause house pressure zones. Common causes of air duct leakage include unsealed connections and panned returns. Air ducts running through unconditioned spaces such as attics, crawlspaces or exterior walls can lose or gain air from outside, or have conditioned air in the air duct tempered by outdoor temperature conditions.

Check(s):
Air Sealed Ducts pg. 46
Check to ensure ducts have either UL 181 water based mastic

or tape on the connection seams. Also, make sure the builder does not install panned supply or return ducts. Alternatively, for existing houses with leaky ducts, you can use AeroSeal® in the duct system to help seal them.

Ducts in conditioned spaces pg. 46
Check attics, unconditioned crawlspaces and exterior walls, including a wall between the house and an unconditioned garage, to ensure you do not have ducts running through them. Alternatively, if you find it economically or aesthetically infeasible to run ducts within conditioned spaces of the house, then you should ensure that you have the duct surrounded by a trough and covered by local code-compliant levels of insulation.

Furniture
Furniture should not block diffusers or registers that supply air to rooms.

Check(s):
High Sidewall Diffusers pg. 48
Check to ensure the HVAC contractor installs high sidewall diffusers so that you will be less likely to block diffusers with furniture.

Unobstructed Diffusers and Registers pg. 48
Check all diffusers and registers in the house to ensure that, where feasible, you do not have furniture blocking air to the rooms.

Pressure Imbalances
Pressure imbalances in the house could cause the conditioning system to work harder and draw make up air from outside through air pathways into the house. This in turn causes increased utility bills and a reduction in comfort. Common causes of pressure imbalances include leaky air ducts, central returns without passage for air to get from rooms to the central return, and operating exhaust fans in the house, including the dryer, without a fresh air intake to the return system.

Check(s):
Transom and Jump Ducts pg. 53
If the house has a central return system, check to ensure you have either a transom or jump duct between the hallway and each room with a door. Note: Houses with central return duct systems do not have return ducts in individual rooms. They instead have a very large return duct located in a hallway.

Air Sealed Air Ducts pg. 46
Check to ensure ducts have either UL 181 water based mastic or tape on the connection seams. Alternatively, for existing houses with leaky ducts you can use AeroSeal® in the duct system to help seal them.

Air Ducts within Conditioned Spaces pg. 46
Check attics, unconditioned crawlspaces and exterior walls, including a wall between the house and a garage, to ensure you do not have ducts running through them. Alternatively, if you find it economically or aesthetically infeasible to run ducts within conditioned spaces of the house, ensure you have the duct surrounded by a trough and covered by local code-compliant levels of insulation.

Conditioning Tests

Flow Hood
The flow hood is an instrument that a Home Energy Rater can place over a diffuser to measure the cubic feet per minute (cfm) of air coming out of it. By taking this measurement and comparing it to the calculated cfm for the room, a Home Energy Rater can tell if the builder installed the duct system according to specifications.

Duct Blaster
Home Energy Raters use duct blasters to measure the air leakage in duct systems. They hook a Home Energy Rater duct blaster fan up to the air handler after blocking all the diffusers and return grilles. They then run the fan to pressurize the system and measure how many cubic feet per minute (cfm)

of air it takes to keep it pressurized. The measured cfm is the leakage rate of the supply ducts, which should be less than 10% of the total air handler fan capacity.

Insulation

Air Ducts
Air ducts running through unconditioned spaces such as attics, crawlspaces or exterior walls can lose or gain air from outside, or have conditioned air in the duct tempered by outdoor temperature conditions.

Check(s):
Air Sealed Ducts pg. 46
Check to ensure ducts have either UL 181 water based mastic or tape on the connection seams. Also, make sure the builder does not install panned supply or return ducts. Alternatively, for existing houses with leaky ducts you can use AeroSeal® in the duct system to help seal them.

Ducts in conditioned spaces pg. 46
Check attics, unconditioned crawlspaces and exterior walls, including a wall between the house and an unconditioned garage, to ensure you do not have ducts running through them. Alternatively, if you find it economically or aesthetically infeasible to run ducts within conditioned spaces of the house, ensure you have the duct surrounded by a trough and covered by local code-compliant levels of insulation.

Attics
Blown-in insulation must evenly cover the attic to the local code compliant level to operate as advertised.

Check(s):
Insulation Gauges pg. 19
Check for insulation gauges and the code compliant depth of insulation in the attic. Insulation gauges assist the insulation installer in obtaining the required depth of insulation throughout

the attic. It also assists you in ensuring the insulation installer evenly covered the entire attic to the code compliant level.

Band Joists
If not insulated correctly, or not insulated at all, band joists will allow heat and air to pass through the entire perimeter of the house.

Check(s):
Insulated and Air Sealed Band Joist pg. 28
Where possible, check the interior side of the band joist to ensure the contractors insulated and air sealed the band joist bays. At a minimum, they should install fiberglass batts into each bay. Optimally, they should spray foam insulation into this area to both insulate and air seal the band joist bays.

Bump-Outs
Bump-out floors should have air sealed and sandwiched insulated floors for draftstopping as well as insulation value.

Check(s):
Insulated Bump-Out Floor pg. 8
Check to ensure the underside of bump-outs has insulation sandwiched between sheathing materials.

Crawlspaces
Crawlspaces should have insulation and air sealing like a well built basement.

Check(s):
Insulated and Air Sealed Crawlspace Access Door pg. 63
If you have an insulated crawlspace, check to make sure the access door is both insulated and air sealed.

Insulated Crawlspace Walls pg. 61
If you have an insulated crawlspace, check to make sure it has the following: 6mm plastic covering the entire ground surface, overlapping and lapping up the sides of the walls and pier pilings at least 6 inches; vents sealed and insulated; band joist

insulated preferably with spray-foam insulation; and passive or active conditioning.

If the crawlspace does not have insulation and you would like to insulate it, you must first gain control of any moisture issue in the crawlspace. In addition, you should install 6mm plastic covering the entire ground surface area, overlapping and lapping up the sides of the walls and pier pilings at least 6 inches; vents sealed and insulated; band joist insulated preferably with spray-foam insulation; and passive or active conditioning.

Fiberglass Wall Insulation
In order for fiberglass insulation to provide its rated insulation value, it must fill each stud bay completely so that no air pockets exist in external walls, including walls between the house and an attached garage.

Check(s):
Completely Filled Stud bays pg. 6
Check to ensure the fiberglass insulation completely fills each stud bay from top to bottom, front to back and side-to-side without being stuffed in or behind anything.

Exterior Wall Outlet Boxes and Light Switch Boxes pg. 25
Check to ensure each stud bay has insulation neatly cut around the outlet and switch boxes in external walls.

Cables and Wires in External Walls pg. 7
Check to ensure each external wall stud bay has insulation neatly cut to envelope cables or wires.

Fireplace Bump-outs
Just like a regular bump-out, a fireplace bump-out must have insulation sandwiched in its walls and floor.

Check(s): Insulated Fireplace Bump-outs pg. 8
Ensure the fireplace bump-out has insulation in its walls and floor, sandwiched in between two sheathing materials.

Foundation Insulation

Foundation walls will transfer heat in or out of the house faster than you may think. Although soil will provide some thermal protection for the foundation, insulating the exterior or interior of the foundation walls will provide even more thermal protection.

Check(s):
Insulated Foundation Walls pg. 61
Check to ensure the foundation wall has either interior or exterior insulation. If it does not and you plan to insulate it, make sure you first gain control of any foundation moisture issues.

Garage and House Common Wall

The garage common wall should not exchange heat or air with the rest of the house.

Check(s):
Insulated and Air Sealed Common Wall pg. 105
Check to ensure the builder insulates and air seals the garage common wall as if it is an exterior wall. Insulating and air sealing the wall includes a continuous bead of glue applied under the bottom plate, completely filled stud bays, continuous bead of glue for the drywall, and gasket type outlet and switch boxes. Alternatively, if you own a pre-existing house you can install a garage-opener-activated exhaust fan in the garage to pull air from the house into the garage instead of the other way around.

Unprotected Insulation

The insulation quality of fiberglass batt insulation degrades by half when not sandwiched in between two pieces of sheathing.

Check(s):
Insulation Sandwich pg. 7
Check to make sure fiberglass insulation in the house has sheathing material on either side of it. Check rooms over

garages, rooms in which attics run on the perimeter between the roof and exterior side of the interior wall and bathtubs against exterior walls. If you can see exposed insulation on the wall, the house does not have an insulation sandwich on this wall.

Wood as Insulation

Wood studs only have a fraction of the insulating properties of actual insulation, and steel studs will transfer heat in or out of the house. Therefore, houses will have better thermal retention properties where builders minimize wood studs on external walls, and cover the exterior side of steel studs with closed cell foam insulation sheathing.

Check(s):
Appropriate Amount of Lumber around Window and Door Frames pg. 17
Check to make sure that the builder only uses the code compliant amount of studs in the house's walls.

Ladder Framing pg. 18
Check for ladder framing where internal walls meet external walls. Ladder framing provides a nailing surface for the interior drywall installer and allows the insulation installer to apply insulation in the stud bay.

Two-Stud Corners pg. 17
Check the intersection of two external walls for a two stud corner framing technique. Two-stud corner framing techniques reduce the amount of lumber used in external walls, and allows the insulation installer to install insulation all the way back into the corner of the wall.

Foam Insulation Sheathing pg. 19
For houses with steel studs in the exterior walls, check to ensure the steel studs have foam insulation sheathing on their exterior side.

Insulation Tests

Unfortunately, the housing industry does not have a measurable method of determining the effectiveness of insulation in houses after the contractors installs drywall. However, you can get a good idea of how well they insulated the house by using a thermal imaging camera. Thermal imaging cameras display surface temperatures of objects they read. By taking thermal images of interior walls, you can view different colors displayed in the picture to determine if the walls have an even distribution of insulation or if they have cold spots.

You can use thermal imaging cameras on any house. Yet, they work best in colder climates during winter where greater temperature differences between the conditioned inside and outside air allow the camera to show you the extremes. Ask a Home Energy Rater about using a thermal imaging camera on your house.

Safety

Atmospherically Vented Gas Appliances

Atmospherically vented gas appliances frequently backdraft due to pressure imbalances in the house. Therefore, the carbon monoxide created by an atmospherically vented gas appliance stays in the house instead of exhausting outside.

Check(s):
Enclosed-Combustion and Power-Vented Gas Appliances pg. 104

If you have gas appliances, check to ensure you have either enclosed-combustion or power-vented gas appliances.

Bathrooms

Bathrooms accumulate a lot of moisture in a concentrated area that can lead to mold problems over time.

Check(s):
Bathroom Vent Fan pg. 89
Check to ensure the bathroom has a vent fan that exhausts to the outside and not to the attic. To automatically run your bathroom vent fan when the humidity reaches a preset level, connect it to a humidistat.

Brick Walls

In a driving rain, brick facades will leak up to 1.5 gallons of water per hour inside the wall for every 12 square feet of brick surface. Therefore, water penetrates behind brick and, if it does not have an easy way to drain out, it will drain to the interior of the house.

Check(s):
Weep Holes pg. 88
Check to ensure the brick façade exterior wall has weep holes every 4 feet at the bottom. Also, check for weep holes over window, door and garage ledges. Weep holes are gaps at the bottom of brick walls and over window, door and garage ledges that allow water to drain out. In a best-case scenario, brick cladding would have air holes at the top and weep holes at the bottom to allow air to flow behind the wall and dry it out faster.

Mortar Catch Screens pg. 88
Check to ensure your builder installs a mortar catch screen between your drainage plane and the brick cladding wall to keep mortar droppings from clogging the weep holes.

Crawlspaces

Moisture gains access to the crawlspace via capillary action on through the footer, evaporation from the ground, crawlspace walls, and via air pathways like the crawlspace vents and band joist. Additionally, you can also get water in the crawlspace via leaking pipes, a rising water table or water run off. This moisture accumulation can lead to excessive mold growth.

Check(s):
Footer Capillary Break pg. 98
Check to ensure you have 6mm plastic laid down underneath the footer, or between the footer and foundation wall to create a capillary break.

Foundation Drainage System pg. 96
Check to ensure:
1. The house has a foundation drain
2. The drain sits as low relative to the footer as structurally feasible
3. The drain moves water away from the house in a down slope direction of at least 1% grade
4. The drain is covered with at least 3 ft of crushed gravel where possible
5. The crushed gravel is wrapped in a silt screen
6. The drain goes to a known location away from the house

Foundation Drainage Planes pg. 96
Check to ensure the foundation wall has a drainage plane to keep water away from the foundation wall and flowing directly into the foundation drain.

Foundation Grading
Check to ensure the ground slopes away from the house at a 5% grade or more to move water away from the house as fast as possible.

Leak Free Pipes pg. 60
Check to ensure that all water carrying pipes running through the crawlspace do not leak.

Sump Pump pg.60
If the house can get flooded or has the potential for a rising water table to accumulate water in the crawlspace, check to make sure you have a sump pit and sump pump installed in the crawlspace with the drainage pipe draining out, down, and away from the house.

Dormers

Dormers are mini roof to sidewall transitions. This is a problem area because water coming down the roof will flow against the sidewall and potentially get into the interior wall cavity where it can cause mold. Additionally, for houses with natural fiber siding, if the cut edge of the siding gets too close to the flashing it can wick moisture into its fibers and release it in a location where moisture will gain entry into the house.

Check(s):
Roof Rake to Sidewall Flashing pg. 81
Check to ensure the roof to sidewall transitions have all roofing layers, housewrap and flashing integrated effectively.

Exposed Flashing pg. 82
Check to ensure you can see at least 1 1/2 inch of flashing between the roof and cut edge of the natural fiber siding.

Drainage Planes

Every exterior cladding system on houses, i.e., vinyl, wood, brick, stucco, shingles, etc., allows water to penetrate behind it. Therefore, the drainage plane must drain bulk water to the bottom of the cladding and then to the outside.

Check(s):
Drainage Plane pg. 86
Check to ensure the housewrap overlaps shingle style with taped seams, starting at the bottom of the house and going up the side.

Garages

Attached and integral garages may have air pathways where potential automobile and solvent contaminated air can find their way into the house. Automobiles emit the most carbon monoxide when you first start them, and can emit carbon monoxide up to 30 minutes after you turn them off. In addition, you may store many hazardous household products in the garage, which could also become airborne contaminants.

Check(s):
Sealed Common Wall pg. 105
Check to ensure you have all air pathways between an attached or integral garage and the rest of the house sealed.

Exterior Grade Door to Garage pg. 105
Check to ensure you have an exterior grade door that provides access between the house and the garage.

Air Handling Units and Air Ducts pg. 106
Check to ensure you do not have air handling units or air ducts running through the garage. If you do, either move them inside the conditioned spaces of the house or move the conditioned spaces of the house to them.

Gutters and Gutter Down-Spouts

Gutters collect water from the roof so that it does not fall next to the foundation and saturate the foundation walls. Additionally, gutter down-spouts provide a path for the collected water in the gutters to drain out and away from the house. Some houses may have gutter down-spouts tied into the foundation drain. This will also saturate the foundation and could lead to moisture damage or mold problems.

Check(s):
Gutters on the House pg. 86
Check to ensure the house has gutters if you live in a rain-prone climate.

Gutter Down-Spouts pg. 86
Check to ensure gutter down-spouts terminate at least 6 feet away from the foundation and drain in a downhill direction away from the house's foundation.

Kitchens

Many kitchens today have re-circulating fans over stoves versus fans that exhaust air to the outside. Re-circulating fans will not remove carbon monoxide or moisture from the kitchen. This can lead to health and mold issues.

Check(s):
Kitchen Exhaust Fan pg. 102
Check to ensure the range hood fan vents to the outside by identifying the range hood exhaust port on the exterior wall.

Ridge Vents

Although ridge vents provide the best method for venting air out of the attic, they also can allow wind driven rain or snow to blow into the attic. This can cause mold growth or moisture spots on ceilings.

Check(s):
Moisture Barrier Ridge Vents pg. 81
Check for ridge vents that have part of its structure turned back up to prevent wind driven rain or snow from entering the vent. If the house does not have a ridge vent, the next time you replace the roof, be sure your roofer installs ridge and soffit vents.

Roof Eaves

In snow-prone climates, roof eaves are susceptible to ice damming, which can lead to their rotting out.

Check(s):
Roof Eave Ice and Water Shield® pg. 82
If you live in a snow prone climate, ensure that you have Ice and Water Shield® installed on the outer surface of your roof over the eaves and under the shingles.

Roof to Sidewall Transitions

Roof to Sidewall Transitions are most commonly seen where a garage roof attaches to the main house. If roofers do not integrate the different roofing layers, flashing and housewrap together properly, water can get into the interior wall. Additionally, for houses with natural fiber siding, if builders install the cut edge of the siding too close to the flashing, the siding can wick moisture into its fibers and release it in a location where the moisture will gain entry into the house.

Check(s):
Roof Rake to Sidewall Flashing pg. 76
Check to ensure the roof to sidewall transitions have stepped flashing that extends at least 2.5 inches up past the cut line of the siding.

Kickout Flashing pg. 50
Check to ensure the roof to sidewall has kick-out flashing at the end of the sidewall to divert bulk water into the gutter, instead of allowing it to converge on the corner of a wall and potentially drain down the exterior wall to the ground.

Exposed Flashing pg. 82
Check to ensure you can see between a half inch to an inch of flashing between the roof and cut edge of the natural fiber siding.

Roofs Sloping Down to a Chimney

Flat surfaces of chimneys, located at the bottom of sloping roofs, do not provide a means for water to drain to either side. Water running down the roof hits the broad side of the chimney, does not drain, and eventually finds its way inside the house.

Check(s):
Crickets pg.77
Check for a properly flashed cricket between the roof and up slope side of the chimney.

Valleys

Valleys create a moisture issue because rain water from the two sides of the roof converges in this location. Rain water can overwhelm this area and potentially get past the shingles, flashing and roofing felt into the attic to cause moisture damage and mold.

Check(s):
Valley Ice and Water Shield® or Roofing felt pg. 77
Check to ensure you have Ice and Water Shield® or roofing felt running up the valley. Also ensure horizontally run roofing felt overlaps and terminates on top of the valley Ice and Water Shield® or roofing felt.

Valley Flashing pg. 77
Check to ensure you have metal flashing running long ways up the valley from the gutter to the roof ridge.

Shingle Cut Line pg. 77
Check to ensure the shingles overlap on, and terminate in the valley flashing.

Ventless Gas Fireplaces
Ventless gas fireplaces release their carbon monoxide by-products into houses versus having a dedicated vent to the outside. Government standards approve the level of carbon monoxide released into houses by these appliances. You need to decide if *any* amount of carbon monoxide released into your house is safe for you or your family.

Check(s):
Direct Vent Gas Fireplaces pg. 106
If you have, or want a gas fireplace in your house, I recommend a direct vent gas fireplace.

Windows
Any penetration through, or protrusion from the exterior wall, such as windows, doors and bay windows, creates a potential water leakage area. Water draining down the drainage plane of an exterior wall can very easily find its way behind a window or door flange and into the interior wall cavity.

Check(s):
Drainage Plane Integration pg. 87
Check to ensure the windows are properly integrated with the house's drainage plane.

Safety Tests

Humidistat

Humidistats are devices that measure the humidity level. Ideally, you should have a humidistat for each floor of the house, especially if you have a basement. ASHRAE standard 55 recommends that you keep the humidity level between 0% and 65%. Since everyone has different levels of comfort, you will need to find your personal comfort zone within those specifications.

Carbon Monoxide Monitors

If you have fossil fuel burning appliances in the house, you should also have a carbon monoxide monitor. Although they are not infallible, they are still a good safeguard.

<u>Ventilation</u>

Airtight Houses

Airtight houses rarely get enough fresh air to replace the stale, polluted air in the house.

Check(s):
Mechanical Ventilation pg. 70
If you have an airtight house, check to ensure the house has some type of mechanical ventilation necessasry to receive the ASHRAE recommended air exchange.

✔	Appendix B Good House Inspection Checklist	
	Check Items	Page #
Foundation		
	Capillary break under footer or between footer and foundation wall or slab if slab on grade	98
	Insulation under concrete floor or slab (optional)	64
	Capillary break under concrete floor or slab	98
	Bituminous coating on exterior of foundation walls	61
	Exterior insulation applied against foundation walls or slab on grade slab edge (optional)	61
	Hydrostatic pressure break applied against foundation walls or slab-on-grade slab edge if not incorporated with exterior insulation	96
	Silt screen in foundation trench	96
	Foundation drain on top of silt screen with at least 1% grade draining to daylight or to appropriate removal system	96
	If enough depth, pour 3 feet of crushed gravel, no fines, over the foundation drain and silt screen. If not enough depth cover foundation drain with as much gravel as possible	96
	Silt screen wrapped completely around gravel to foundation wall	96
	Foam sill sealer between the foundation wall and foundation wall sill plate	28
Framing		
	Bottom plate gasket between sub-floor or slab and exterior wall frame for each floor	28
	2-stud corners at intersections of two exterior walls	17
	Ladder Framing at intersections of interior and exterior walls	18
	Appropriate amount of lumber used around window and door frames	17

✔	Check Items	Page #
Roofing		
	Moisture barrier ridge vent installed on roof ridge	81
	Soffit vents underneath roof eave	82
	Ice and Water Shield or roofing paper in valleys from gutter to roof ridge	77
	Horizontally run roofing paper applied shingle style, overlapped and terminated on valley roofing paper	77
	Sheet metal flashing in valleys from gutter to roof ridge	77
	Cricket between up slope side of chimney and roof	77
	Cricket step flashed to chimney, see Step Flashing	82
	Step flashing against roof rake to sidewall transitions and dormers	81
	Step flashing cut into mortar joints on brick cladding	82
	Flashing extends at least 2.5 inches up past the cladding lip that covers it	76
	Ice and Water Shield applied on roof over eves (colder climates only)	82
	Inch and a half of exposed flashing at roof rake to sidewall transition if using natural fiber siding	81
	Kickout flashing at bottom of roof rake to sidewall transition	82
Drainage Plane		
	Housewrap applied shingle style and overlapped going up side of house	87
	Housewrap horizontal and vertical seams taped	87
	All windows, doors and other protrusions from exterior wall integrated into drainage plane	87
	Weep holes every 4 feet at the bottom of brick cladding	88
	Weep holes over window, door and garage door ledges on brick houses	88

✔	Check Items	Page #
Drainage Plane Cont'd		
	Mortar catch screens installed between drainage plane and brick cladding walls	88
	Air holes at the top of brick cladding (optional)	88
	Stucco weep screed installed at least 4 inches above finished grade and at least two inches above concrete walkway or other hard surface on stucco walls.	89
	Gutters or other water directing method installed on your house	86
	Gutter down spouts independent and separate from French drain	86
	Gutter down spouts terminate at least 6 feet away from the house and drain in a down hill direction away from the house.	86
HVAC		
	Calculated room to room air flows based on volume of room, insulation R-value in walls, total surface area of windows, U-value of windows and cardinal orientation of room	43
	Equivalent length calculations for each air duct run	43
	Air ducts inside conditioned spaces of house i.e., no air ducts in attic, unconditioned crawlspaces, garages or exterior walls including common wall between house and garage	46
	Fully ducted supply and return air duct system i.e. no panned air ducts	48
	Air ducts air sealed with UL181 approved water based mastic or tape	46
	Balanced, exhaust-only or supply-only fresh air system for airtight houses	70
	High sidewall diffusers i.e. no diffusers low on a wall, under a window or on a floor	49
	Transom or jump ducts to rooms with doors if house has a central return	53

✔	Check Items	Page #
Crawlspace		
	Capillary break under footer or between footer and foundation wall	98
	Bituminous coating on exterior of foundation walls	61
	Exterior insulation applied against foundation walls (optional)	61
	Hydrostatic pressure break applied against foundation walls if not incorporated with exterior insulation	96
	Silt screen in foundation trench	96
	Foundation drain on top of silt screen with at least 1% grade draining to daylight or to appropriate removal system	96
	If enough depth, pour 3 feet of crushed gravel, no fines, over the foundation drain and silt screen. If not enough depth cover foundation drain with as much gravel as possible.	96
	Silt screen wrapped completely around gravel to foundation wall	96
	No leaky pipes in crawlspace	60
	6mm plastic completely covering ground, overlapping from sheet to sheet and lapping up sides of walls	60
	No air vents in crawlspace	57-58
	Interior crawlspace walls insulated if exterior insulation not installed	63
	Band joist insulated and air sealed	28
	Crawlspace access door insulated and air sealed	63
	Radiant barrier on bottom of crawlspace floor (optional)	58
	Passively or actively conditioned crawlspace	61
Insulation		
	Band joist insulated and air sealed	28

✔	Check Items	Page #
Insulation Cont'd		
	Rough opening between windows and framing and doors and framing sealed with low expansion spray foam	27
	Stud bays completely filled with fiberglass insulation i.e. no air gaps or potential air pockets	6
	Fiberglass insulation neatly cut around outlet and light switch boxes in exterior wall stud bays	7
	Fiberglass insulation neatly cut to encapsulate electric cable running through exterior walls	7
	Gasket type or foam sealed outlet and light switch boxes in exterior walls	25
	Penetrations through exterior walls filled with spray foam	27
	Common wall between house and garage treated like an exterior wall	105
	Bump-outs have air sealed and insulated floors	8
	Fireplace insert bump-outs have insulated and air sealed walls and floor	8
	Interior basement walls insulated if exterior insulation not installed	63
	Continuous bead of glue on studs before attaching drywall to exterior walls and ceilings	25
	All insulated walls have sheeting material on both sides including rooms over garages, rooms beside attic spaces and behind bathtubs installed against exterior walls	7
	Attic insulation evenly applied to local code compliant depth	19
Carbon Monoxide		
	Kitchen range hood fan exhausts to outside	102
	Fossil Fuel burning appliances are either sealed combustion or power-vented i.e. no atmospherically vented fossil fuel burning appliances	104

✔	Check Items	Page #
	Carbon Monoxide Cont'd	
	Exhaust fan in garage operated by garage door opener (optional)	106
	Fireplace inserts are direct vented i.e. no ventless gas fireplaces	106
	Interior Moisture Control	
	Kitchen range hood fan exhausts to the outside	89
	Bathroom vent fan exhausts to the outside, i.e. does not terminate in attic	89
	Bathroom vent fan connected to humidistat (optional)	90
	Air Pathways	
	Enclosed recess lights	26
	Door to garage is an exterior grade door	105
	No open hearth fireplaces (optional)	65

Appendix C
Construction Glossary

A

air diffuser

An outlet in an air supply duct for distributing and blending air in an enclosure. Usually a round, square or rectangular unit mounted in a suspended ceiling.

air-handling unit (AHU)

The traditional method of heating, cooling, and ventilating a building by which single- or variable-speed fans push air over hot or cold coils, then through dampers and ducts and into one or more rooms.

air leakage

The air that escapes from a system or enclosure through cracks, joints, and couplings.

ASHRAE

American Society of Heating, Refrigeration and Air-Conditioning Engineers.

B

balancing damper

A plate or adjustable vane installed in a duct branch to regulate the flow of air in the duct.

band joist

A vertical member that forms the perimeter of a floor system.

basement

The bottom full story of a building below the first floor. A basement may be partially or completely below grade.

batt insulation	Thermal or sound insulating material, such as fiberglass or expanded shale, which has been fashioned into a flexible, blanket-like form, often with a vapor barrier on one side. Batt insulation is manufactured in dimensions that facilitate its installation between the studs or joists of a frame construction.
bay	In construction, the space between two main trusses or beams.
bituminous coating	Any waterproof or protective coating whose base is a compound of asphalt or tar.
blocking	Small pieces of wood used to secure, join, or reinforce members, or to fill spaces between members.
board insulation (insulating board, insulation board)	Lightweight thermal insulation, such as polystyrene, manufactured in rigid or semi-rigid form, whose thickness is very small relative to other dimensions. Board insulation offers little structural strength, and is usually applied under a finish material, although some types are surface-finished on one side.
bottom plate	See sill

C

cfm, CFM	cubic feet per minute
capillary action	In subsurface soil conditions, the rising of water above the horizontal plane of the water table.

capillary break	A water impervious material placed between a moisture laden surface and a surface that absorbs moisture, to prevent moisture transferring from one substance to the other.
cavity	The empty space between studs and joists
central air	A system that contains a central boiler, furnace or heat pump to heat or cool air and ductwork to distribute the conditioned air.
chimney	A vertical, noncombustible structure with one or more flues to carry smoke and other gases of combustion into the atmosphere.
chimney cricket	A small false roof built behind a chimney on the main roof to divert rainwater away from the chimney.
chimney flue	A vertical passageway in a chimney through which the hot gases flow. A chimney may contain one or several flues. Flues are typically lined with fired clay pipes to resist corrosion and facilitate cleaning.
chase	A continuous enclosure in a structure that acts as a housing for pipe, wiring conduits, ducts, etc. A chase is usually located in or adjacent to a column, which provides some physical protection.

cladding

A covering or sheathing applied to provide desirable surface properties, such as durability, weathering, aesthetics*, and corrosion or impact resistance.

closed-cell

A type of foamed material in which each cell is totally enclosed and separate so that the bulk of the material will not soak up liquid like a sponge. Closed-cell material is characteristic of certain types of insulation board and flexible glazing gaskets.

cripple

In construction framing, members that are less than full length; for example, studs above a door or below a window.

D

damper

A blade or louver within an air duct, inlet, or outlet that can be adjusted to regulate the flow of air. (2) A pivotal cast-iron plate positioned just below the smoke chamber of a fireplace to regulate drafts.

detail

A large scale architectural or engineering drawing indicating specific configurations and dimensions of construction elements. If the large-scale drawing differs from the general drawing, it is the architect's or engineer's intention that the large-scale drawing be used to clarify the general drawing.

dewpoint	(1) The temperature at which air of a given moisture content becomes saturated with water vapor. (2) The temperature at which the relative humidity of the air is 100%.
diffuser	A circular, square or rectangular air distribution outlet, generally located in the ceiling and comprised of deflecting members to discharge supply air in various directions.
dormer	A projection through the slope of a roof for a vertical window.
drywall	Interior finish construction materials that are manufactured and installed in preformed sheets, such as gypsum wallboard. Drywall is an alternative to plaster.
duct	In HVAC systems, the conduit used to distribute the air.
duct system	The connected elements of an air-distribution system through ductwork.
ductwork	The ducts of an HVAC system.

E

EEBA	Energy and Environmental Building Association
eave	(1) Those portions of a roof that project beyond the outside walls of a building. (2) The bottom edges of a sloping roof.

F

fiberglass	Filaments of glass formed by pulling molten glass into random lengths that are either gathered into a wool-like mass or formed as continuous threads. The wool-like form is used as thermal or acoustical insulation. The thread-like form is used as reinforcing material and in textiles, glass fabrics, and electrical insulation.
flashing	A thin, impervious sheet of material placed in construction to prevent water penetration or direct the flow of water. Flashing is used especially at roof hips and valleys, roof penetrations, joints between roof and a vertical wall, and in masonry walls to direct the flow of water and moisture.
flue	A noncombustible and heat-resistant passage in a chimney used to convey products of combustion from a furnace fireplace or boiler to the atmosphere.
footing	That portion of the foundation of a structure that spreads and transmits the load directly to the soil.
framing	Structural timbers assembled into a given construction system.

G

grade	The surface or level of the ground.

gutter	A shallow channel of wood, metal, or PVC positioned just below and following along the eaves of a building for the purpose of collecting and diverting water from a roof.

H

HVAC	heating, ventilating, and air-conditioning
hearth	The floor of a fireplace and the adjacent area of fireproof material.
heat pump	A refrigeration system designed to utilize alternately or simultaneously the heat extracted at a low temperature and the heat rejected at a higher temperature.
header	see lintel
high efficiency particulate air filter (HEPA filter)	A high-efficiency (99.9%) dry filter made in an extended surface configuration of deep space folds on submicron glass fiber paper.
humidity	The water vapor contained in a given space, area or environment.

I

ice dam	An accumulation of ice and snow at the eaves of a sloping roof.
insulation	Material used to reduce the effects of heat, cold or sound.

K

king stud — In framing, a vertical support member that extends from the bottom to top plate alongside an opening for a door or window.

L

lintel — A horizontal supporting member, installed above an opening such as a window or a door, that serves to carry the weight of the wall above it.

M

mildew — A fungus that grows on damp fabric and other materials, particularly when there is a lack of air circulation.

O

on center — A measurement of the distance between the centers of two repeating members in a structure.

oriented strand board (OSB) — Panels made of narrow strands of wood fiber oriented lengthwise and crosswise in layers, with a resin binder. Depending on the resin used, OSB can be suitable for interior or exterior applications.

R

rake — To slant or incline from the vertical or horizontal.

register — An opening to a room or space for the passage of conditioned air. The register has a grill and a damper for flow regulation.

ridge vent	A vent installed along the top ridge of a roof to permit air to pass from* the attic or the peak of a cathedral ceiling.

S

screed	A strip of wood, plaster, or metal placed on a wall or pavement as a guide for the even application of plaster or concrete.
sheathing	The first covering of exterior studs or rafters by boards, plywood or particle board.
sill	(1) The horizontal member of the bottom of a window or exterior door frame. (2) As applied to general construction, the lowest member of the frame of the structure, resting on the foundation and supporting the frame.
slab	A flat, horizontal (or nearly horizontal) molded layer of plain or reinforced concrete, usually of uniform but sometimes of variable thickness, positioned either on the ground or supported by beams, columns, walls, or other framework.
soffit	The underside of a part or member of a structure, such as a beam, a stairway, or arch.
step flashing	Individual small pieces of metal flashing material used to flash around chimneys, dormers, and such projections along the slope of a roof. The individual pieces are overlapped and stepped up the vertical surface.

stud	A framing member, usually cut to a precise length at the mill, designed to be used in framing building walls with little or no trimming before it is set in place. Studs are most often 2"x 4", but 2"x 3" or 2"x 6" and other sizes are also included in the stud category. Studs may be of wood, steel or composite material.
stud bay	The empty space between studs.

T

top plate	A member on top of a stud wall on which joists rest to support an additional floor or to form a ceiling.

V

voc	volatile organic compound
valley	A place where two planes of a roof meet at a downward, or "V", angle.

Appendix D
Resource Directory

Air Pathway Inhibitors

Gasket outlet and switch boxes	http://www.lessco-airtight.com www.sheltersupply.com
Airtight recessed lights	http://www.pegasusassociates.com http://www.lampsontheweb.com http://oikos.com http://www.elights.com

Direct Vent Fireplaces

Heat'n Glo	http://www.heatnglo.com
Pellet Stoves	http://www.harmanstoves.com http://www.quadrafire.com http://www.thelinco.com
Stone Wood Stoves	http://www.woodstove.com http://www.hearthstonestoves.com

Drainage Plane

Peel & Stick™	http://www.genflex.com
R-Wrap®	http://www.ludlowcp.com
Typar®	http://www.typarhousewrap.com
Tyvek®	http://www.tyvek.com
Weep Screeds	http://www.vinylcorp.com http://amico-lath.com

Duct Systems

UL 181 Mastic	http://www.hardcast.com; http://rcdcorp.com
UL 181 Tape	http://poseysupply.com
IBACOS Duct Designs	http://www.ibacos.com
AeroSeal®	http://www.aeroseal.com
AirCycler™	http://www.aircycler.com

Enclosed-Combustion and Power-Vented Appliances

Furnaces and Water Heaters	http://mctg.phpwebhosting.com/gama/

Exterior Doors

All Seasons Window & Door	http://www.allseasonswindows.com
CWD Windows and Doors	http://www.cwdwindows.com

Exterior Doors Cont'd

EAGLE Window and
Door, Inc.   http://www.eaglewindow.com

Feather River Door
Company   http://www.featherriverdoors.com

Gerkin Windows and
Doors   http://www.gerkin.com

Marvin Windows and
Doors   http://www.marvin.com

Pella   http://www.pella.com

Precision Entry, Inc.   http://www.precisionentry.com

Showcase Windows and
Doors   http://www.showcasewindows.com/main.html

Therma-Tru   http://www.thermatru.com

Windor, Inc.   http://www.tritondoor.com

Flexible Sheathing

Energy Brace®   http://www.ludlowcp.com

Thermo Ply®   http://www.ludlowcp.com

Foundation Drainage Plane

Dow Styrofoam Building
Materials   http://www.dow.com

Enkadrain®   http://www.colbond-geosynthetics.com

Foundation Insulation

Basement Wall and
Masonry Wall Fiber Glass
Building Insulation   http://www.certainteed.com/CertainTeed

Dow Styrofoam Building
Materials   http://www.dow.com

Owens Corning Insulation
Products   http://www.owenscorning.com

Foil faced rigid insulation www.radiantbarrier.com
                             http://astrofoil.net

Framing Materials

Drywall Clips   http://www.prest-on.com; http://www.thenailer.com

Sill Gasket   http://www.raindrains.com
                             http://www.owenscorning.com; http://www.dow.com

Roofing Products

Ice and Water Shield®	http://www.alliedbuilding.com
Ridge Vent	http://www.airvent.com http://www.owenscorning.com
Dow Styrofoam Building Materials	http://www.dow.com

Spray Foam Insulation

CorBond®	http://www.corbond.com
Icynene®	http://www.icynene.com
Window & Door low expansion spray foam	http://greatstuff.dow.com

Ventilation Systems

ERV	http://www.broan.com http://www.carrierresidential.com
HRV	http://www.broan.com http://www.carrierresidential.com
HEPA Filters	http://www.broan.com

Miscellaneous Websites

Building Codes	http://www.global.ihs.com
Builders Guides	http://www.eeba.org
General Information	http://www.buildiq.com http://www.buildingscience.com http://www.eere.energy.gov/buildings/building_america/about.html http://www.yourgoodhouse.com
Home Energy Raters	http://www.natresnet.org

Index

(E cont'd)

equivalent length 43, 118, 137
ERV 73-74, 153
exhaust fan 71-72, 89, 116, 124, 131, 140
exterior insulation 61, 98, 111, 124, 135, 138-139

F

fiberglass 6-7, 17-19, 25-29, 57, 63, 111, 152
fireplace 8, 9, 65-68, 107, 116, 123, 133, 139, 140, 144-147
fireplace bump-outs 9, 123
flashing 61-62, 77-88, 93, 97, 129, 131-133, 136, 146, 149
floor joist 8, 28, 37, 48, 50, 57-58, 63, 105
foundation 8, 28, 30, 60-65, 76, 86, 89, 95-99, 109, 111, 115, 124, 128, 130, 135, 138, 146, 149, 152
furniture 48, 52, 54, 119

G

garage 5, 46, 76, 81, 88, 104-106, 114, 116, 119-124, 127-131, 136-140
gas appliances 102, 104, 126
gas fireplace 68, 107, 116, 133
ground moisture 60
gutter 77, 82, 86, 130, 132-133, 136-137, 147

H

heat pump 39, 41, 143, 147
heat recovery ventilator 73
HEPA filter 74, 147, 153
housewrap 25, 76-82, 85-88, 92-93, 129, 131, 136
HRV 73, 74, 153
hydrostatic pressure 95, 135, 138

I

ice damming 82, 131
insulation cavity 6
insulation sandwich 7-9, 15-16, 122-125
insulation value 7, 43, 122-123
interior insulation 63

J

jump duct 53, 55, 120, 137

K

kickout flashing 82, 132, 136

T

tab-less insulation batt 7, 11
tape 44, 46, 87-88, 93, 115, 118-119 120-121, 137, 151
termite 30, 61-62
thermal bridge 18
top plate 20, 28, 116-117, 148, 150
transom duct 53, 56
trough 46-47, 77, 81, 119-121
two-stud corner 17, 21, 125, 135

U

unconditioned space 26-27, 44-46, 54, 118, 121

V

valley 77-78, 80, 132-133, 136, 150
vent 57-59, 60-61, 68, 70-73, 78, 81-83, 89, 102, 106-107, 116, 122-123, 126-127,
        131, 133, 136, 139, 140, 149, 151, 153
ventilation system 2, 69, 73, 74, 109, 113
ventless gas fireplace 107

W

water heater 103, 104
weep holes 88, 127, 136
weep screed 88-89, 137
window 5, 8, 17, 26-27, 43, 49, 65, 69, 76, 87-90, 93, 117, 127, 133-139, 144-145,
        148-149, 151-153
window flashing 87, 93
wire 27, 114
wood as insulation 17, 125

Author Bio

Matt Shipley has had a lifelong passion for building energy independent houses and has spent many years gleaning information from books and articles that helped shed light on this subject. Matt received a Bachelor of Economics Degree from the United States Naval Academy and served for a total of eleven years on active duty with the United States Navy. He worked for a General Electric Capital company as a process improvement expert before joining a residential construction research firm. During his tenure at the research firm, he participated in cutting edge home performance research and field studies. He currently lives in PA with his wife, the Squawker, and their pets. He continually strives to improve their house to meet the Good House standards.

Good House Bad House is a highly illustrated, easy to read book that will help you understand:

Understand
how to make your house
more Comfortable, Healthy,
Safe, Durable, and Energy Efficient

Matt Shipley

- How to control mold in your house
- Why rooms in your house may be hot in the summer and cold in the winter
- How much ventilation your house needs to provide fresh, clean, breathable air
- Why combustion appliances in your house can be harmful to you
- How you can reduce your energy bills and still comfortably condition your house
- Why an open hearth fireplace actually cools a house instead of heating it
- How you can prevent moisture from getting into your basement
- And more...

Matt Shipley is a building enthusiast who traveled across the United States for a residential construction research company, enlightening production builders about building better houses. He brings this hard to find knowledge to you, the homeowner, for your understanding of how your house works and how you can make it work better.

Published by Maximus Press, Inc.
Cover design by www.stickman-studio.com

ORDER FORM
http://www.yourgoodhouse.com

Yes, I want _____ copies of Good House Bad House at $14.95 each plus $3.49 shipping per book.

My check or money order for $_____is enclosed. Make check payable to:
Maximus Press, Inc.
PO Box 382
Ingomar, PA 15127

Name_____

Address:_____

City/State/Zip: _____

Phone: _____Fax: _____

Email: _____

All Sales Final, No Returns or Refunds